Also by Cecile R. Bauer

Mumma's Favorite
A Lorena McGee Mystery
Yellowback Mysteries, 2008

Justice for Daddy's Little Girl
A Lorena McGee Mystery
Yellowback Mysteries (Fall/Winter 2009)

Stepping Stones
Meditations and Prayers for Spiritual Renewal
Paulist Press, 1999

Caregiver's Gethsemane
Practical and Spiritual Help for Caregivers to the Dying
Paulist Press, 1995

Escape to Sun City
Old Fogies on Motorcycles Rob A Bank and Head West
Northwest Publishing, 1989 / Books in Motion, 2001

Angels Get No Respect
Humorous Tales of Angels on Earth
Magnificat Press, 1987

Mona/Lu
Help and Healing for Parents with Anger Issues
Magnificat, 1987

Trust God
and

CHERISH EVERY MOMENT

Cecile R. Bauer

Cherish Every Moment

CECILE R. BAUER

SEABOARD PRESS

JAMES A. ROCK & COMPANY, PUBLISHERS

Cherish Every Moment by Cecile R. Bauer

SEABOARD PRESS

is an imprint of JAMES A. ROCK & CO., PUBLISHERS

Cherish Every Moment copyright ©2009 by Cecile R. Bauer

With excerpts from David Bauer, Sr.

Special contents of this edition copyright ©2009 by Seaboard Press

Cover Photo: (back row): Cathy, 10; Davy, 11; Rusty, 9; Barb, 8
(front row): Rose, 5; Tom, 3; Mike, 1 (in highchair); Jason, 4; Jean, 7
Point of heart: Jim, age 5, who was not born when the main photo was taken.

Address comments and inquiries to:
SEABOARD PRESS
900 South Irby Street, #508
Florence, SC 29501

E-Mail:
jrock@rockpublishing.com   lrock@rockpublishing.com
Internet URL: www.rockpublishing.com

Trade Paperback ISBN-13/EAN: 978-1-59663-740-5

Library of Congress Control Number: 2008939900

Printed in the United States of America

First Edition: 2009

To

all our

family and friends

May you live long,

love well,

and

Cherish Every Moment

Contents

Prologue .... *xiii*

CHAPTER 1
Come! And Bring Peaches! *1*

CHAPTER 2
How We Began (The Dance) *6*

CHAPTER 3
That Memorable First Kiss *23*

CHAPTER 4
Dating Mishaps: the Good Night Echo *27*

CHAPTER 5
Evening in Paris *31*

CHAPTER 6
The Miracle of Birth *34*

CHAPTER 7
Real Baby Buggies *40*

CHAPTER 8
The Rosary Bread *43*

CHAPTER 9
The Lean Years *48*

CHAPTER 10
Go Fly a Kite *51*

CHAPTER 11
Wish You Were Here *54*

CHAPTER 12
Shoe Store Blues *60*

CHAPTER 13
Cooking Lessons, One through Ten *64*

CHAPTER 14
The Feeding and Nourishing of a Large Family *72*

CHAPTER 15
The Incredible Chili Sit-in and Other Table Talk *77*

CHAPTER 16
Learning the Lesson *81*

CHAPTER 17
Going Down North *85*

CHAPTER 18
The Sea Change *89*

CHAPTER 19
Boil a Kettle *94*

CHAPTER 20
Tommy Tippy and Fishing for Pike *96*

CHAPTER 21
Fishing Poles, Loved and Lost *101*

CHAPTER 22
The Oasis *106*

CHAPTER 23
Tom, Help! *110*

CHAPTER 24
Teaching Drivers' Ed, the Home Edition *114*

CHAPTER 25
Tree House Mishaps *120*

CHAPTER 26
All the Way to D.C. with Singing Sis *123*

CHAPTER 27
Wearry's Mad *128*

CHAPTER 28
The Fye Fazzer and Other Weird Family Labels *134*

CHAPTER 29
Cucumbers and Cards *138*

CHAPTER 30
That Fearsome "F" Word *144*

CHAPTER 31
The Eyeball Cup and Other Family Favorites 149

CHAPTER 32
Freeze-dried Diapers and Other Rituals of Antiquity 153

CHAPTER 33
Vicks, Goose Grease, and Mustard Plasters 157

CHAPTER 34
Oddball Anniversaries that End in Zero 162

CHAPTER 35
Our Electrical Ghost and Other Family Myths 165

CHAPTER 36
Sarge the Wonder Dog 170

CHAPTER 37
Boys into Men 174

CHAPTER 38
Boys, the Middle Years 178

CHAPTER 39
Girls into Grandmas 186

CHAPTER 40
Sierra Smiles 191

CHAPTER 41
Johnny Two-Hat 194

CHAPTER 42
Carole, Grace Under Fire 199

CHAPTER 43
Smoky, the Long Necked Pup 201

CHAPTER 44
Stinky Feet 206

CHAPTER 45
The Rise 210

CHAPTER 46
Mother's Rhubarb Stash 214

CHAPTER 47
So This is Paradise *221*

CHAPTER 48
Maya and Sierra, Babes into Toddlers *224*

CHAPTER 49
The Return of the Prodigal *226*

CHAPTER 50
Miracle Moments to Remember *230*

Blest are We *237*

Photographs

Barbara, Jean, Rose, Davy, Cathy, Rusty, page 63

Baby Jim, page 83

Brother Jimbo, page 125

Larry and Anna, page 131

Dave on motorcycle, page 147

JR falls asleep standing up, page 150

Cecile and brother Jimbo, page 159

Boys of summer, page 185

Carole and John Smith, page 198

My mother, enjoying herself, page 220

Prologue

What does the phrase mean, "Cherish Every Moment?"

Is it some pie in the sky wishful thinking? A myth propagated by church leaders? Some Pollyanna type lifestyle that ignores the challenges of surviving today's real world of war, civil unrest and terrorism? How can anyone survive in today's stress-laden world when your previously calm existence hits the wall? How do you cherish every moment while struggling with serious crises such as unemployment, divorce, homelessness, mind-numbing illness, or the death of a loved one?

When bad things happen to good people, our first thought may very well be, *"O God! Help me!"* We know, within our anguished hearts, that only God has the answer to our deepest fears. *Cherish Every Moment* is God's whisper in the ear of every frightened believer. It is meant as a gentle reminder to pause along our life's journey and give thanks for those moments when God's love is revealed in various, surprising ways.

Cherish Every Moment

is God's whisper

into the ear

of every

frightened believer.

CHAPTER 1

Come!
And Bring Peaches!

As a child of the 1940's, I spent a lot of time in bed, suffering from all the various illnesses of childhood. Measles, Chicken Pox, I caught everything, even Whooping Cough, a double dose that kept me sick and near death for twelve weeks. As I languished in bed, not caring, not eating, the only food that piqued my nonexistent appetite was the irresistible golden slices of my mother's home-canned peaches. Just the sight of those pale yellow slices conjured up fond memories of a hot summertime kitchen, my mother's soft face, misted with perspiration as she bent over the stove, and the irresistible fragrance of peaches fresh from the scalding bath. Home-canned peaches could heal anything from pneumonia to a broken heart, we believed. Whenever anyone in my birth family fell ill, the call went out, *"Come! And bring peaches."* The mysterious healing properties of canned peaches always made us feel better.

Fast forward fifty years. We were living on the West Coast, my husband Dave and me, 2,500 miles away from the majority of our adult children and my elderly mother. We had taken early retirement and gone west to live the easy life in the wonderful sunshine of California. We were too young for Social Security, but his pension from New York State paid our bills. He worked a part-time job to keep busy and I stayed home and wrote books. It was our dream life, something we had planned for many years, and thoroughly enjoyed. Then something terrible happened. Dave's heart began to fail.

It began slowly. He just seemed extra tired in the evenings when he returned from his truck driving job. Born on a farm, Dave loves the outdoors. Each evening, after supper, he would go outside and putter around with the flowers and lawn. He prided himself on having the best kept yard in our mobile home park. But as time went by, he grew more and more fatigued. Instead of going outside after supper, he would collapse in his recliner and sleep the evening away. Then he started calling in sick, spending his days resting instead of working. His recliner became his second home. The yard suffered. Grass began to look brittle from lack of water. I tried enticing him outdoors, thinking the fresh air might help perk up his sagging spirits. He sat on the porch, directing my efforts with the hose, calling out instructions about beheading the roses. His voice sounded frail, old. Dave was only 57, too young to be so weak. Even walking the dog exhausted him. Something was seriously wrong. I made an appointment for him with our HMO.

Dave hated to admit he needed a doctor's help. Farmer boys don't go to the doctor just because they feel tired! The last time he needed a doctor's attention happened at age sixteen when a horseshoe nail ripped a hole in his leg. Even then, he only went for the necessary stitches because his father insisted (plus the amount of blood flowing down his leg made him keel over!). He was no longer that tough farm boy. I had to morph into a nagging parent before he reluctantly gave in and consented to the doctor's appointment.

When you belong to an HMO, you get whatever doctor is available. The doctor on call was a young, strident female doctor. She kept her hands in the pocket of her white smock as she barked out orders. Maybe she was new and she hid her hands to hide their trembling? She had little or no sympathetic bedside manner. Before either of us could grasp the frightening thought that Dave's heart was endangered, she ordered an ambulance for Dave. He was whisked away to the Emergency Room of the local hospital, Kaiser-Permanente. Dave did not go willingly. He flung his shirt on the floor in a high tantrum, scowling his protest, then finally laid back, glowering at everyone around him.

I followed the ambulance. My mind felt completely numb. In the ER, no one seemed alarmed; no one offered comfort to us in what, in our inexperienced minds, was a life-threatening crisis. Dave's heart? Endangered? *Oh God! What can I do?*

God gifts me with a certain calmness whenever the bottom drops out of my life. Outwardly, I am serene, a smile frozen on my stiff face. Inside, I am numb, with a coldness that makes me shiver. I smiled and held Dave's hand while the Emergency Room doctors worked to stabilize his erratic heartbeat. They took a multitude of blood tests, several X-rays, and hooked him up to a heart monitoring machine. I smiled to calm my frightened husband, but inside me, the refrain kept drumming like my own thundering heartbeat.

Oh God, oh God, oh God! What can I do? What can I do now?

After hours of tests and uncertainty, the doctors sent me home. "Nothing more you can do here tonight, Mrs. Bauer. You might as well go home and get some rest. We will call you if there is any change."

Home to a suddenly lonely place. Dog Ginger waiting to be walked, but it was dark, and too late to roam the streets of California. Too dangerous. I felt surrounded by unseen danger. Home, away from the need to put up the front of calmness that Dave needed from me in the hospital, I literally fell apart.

Oh God, oh God, oh God! What can I do? What can I do now?

I telephoned my elderly mother in Western New York. "Come, and bring peaches," I pleaded. My mother, in her 80's, half-blind from cataracts, booked the next flight, and arrived the following morning, with a jar of canned peaches in her carry-on luggage. My mother didn't even own a canner anymore. She gave it to me years ago. Yet, somehow, she secured a jar of home-canned peaches. She handed the jar to me as she arrived at the sunny Sacramento airport. Mother's eyes blinked as she recognized me through the fog of her dim sight. Her hug alone could heal any illness. But that was the next day. The night before, after phoning Mother, my litany of fear continued.

Oh God, oh God, oh God! What can I do? What can I do now?

What if Dave died? What if he needed open heart surgery? Years of recovery? What if he came home an invalid? How would I cope with a farmer boy confined to the house? What if he died?

Oh God, oh God, oh God! What can I do? What can I do now?

My restless mind continued down its path of pessimism. Relentlessly it reviewed the darkness of my limited future without Dave as breadwinner. I was too young for Social Security benefits. Dave's pension ended at his death. How would I manage the bills? Who would hire a freelance writer with limited success? No bestseller or blockbuster novel in my immediate future. My job resume consisted of numerous part-time, minimum wage jobs. I was in my mid-fifties. Who would hire me? Would we lose our home? Would I have to move in with my mother back East? How would that work out? Two women, too much alike to live together in harmony, trying to survive on Mother's limited income? Nightmare time! I fell asleep with my new mantra echoing in my frightened soul.

Oh God, oh God, oh God! What can I do? What can I do now?

Then God gifted me with the dream. In my dream, I wept, tears of pain, tears of fear. They wet my pillow and shook me to my core.

Oh God, oh God, oh God! What can I do? What can I do now?

And God answered, *"Cherish Every Moment."*

As the answer echoed through my fear-filled soul, I felt the arms of the One who died for us. *Jesus hugged me!* He wrapped his arms around me from behind. I tried to see His face but it was hidden. I felt the scratchiness of a beard, the rough material of homespun cloth. Turning my head I caught a glimpse of red whiskers. The hug grew tighter, as wave after wave of peace flooded my very being. It was indescribably sweet, comforting, and filled with endless love.

"My child. *Cherish Every Moment."*

I awoke to tears of relief, and the ringing of the telephone. Leaping up I picked up the receiver, ready for anything or anyone. Good news? Bad news? It didn't matter. *Jesus hugged me!*

"Hi Honey," Dave said, his cheerful voice like sweet music in my ear. "The doctors set me free. Pick me up at the ER entrance, OK? Bring Ginger along. It's too dangerous for you to drive alone in the city at night."

He laughed at my reply. "Dave, after tonight, I am afraid of nothing!"

Turned out that Dave's heart problem was a medication error. The doctor adjusted his medication and he went back to work. The lawn never looked better. Mother had a good visit with us. She even liked the dog, a first for her. The peaches were delicious. And I learned a valuable lesson.

Cherish Every Moment.

Works for me.

CHAPTER 2

❧❧❦❧❧

How We Began
(The Dance)

David

As a poor farm boy growing up in the 1940's, taking time off from the same old everyday chores just to have some fun didn't happen that often. But when I reached my late teens, my friend Huck and I started going to the local square dances. The Wolbert brothers, Ed, Skip, Jerve, and Jim, played for the dances on alternating weeks at the dance halls of Crown and Shippenville. They also played for special dances such as the Fourth of July dance at Lucinda and the Labor Day dance at St. Michael's in Fryburg.

We went in Huck's car, a 1936 black Chevy. He bought the car with money saved up from his job at Walter's Sawmill. After I turned eighteen, Huck got me a job there too. I was saving up for my own car, even thought Huck said I didn't need to.

"I'll take you any place you want to go, Dave," he said and meant it too. He was like that, generous and friendly and not afraid to spend his money.

We were always broke. Fifty cents an hour working at the sawmill part time meant barely enough money for gas and girls. Huck and I each had a girlfriend living over near Marble. We picked them up every Saturday evening and took them to Clarion to the show. After the movies, we treated them to ice cream or hamburgers at a nearby diner.

One week, when the mill had been shut down for three days while they fixed a broken saw, we didn't have enough money to take the girls out to eat after the show. We tried to explain. Huck even made up a song about, "No Money in My Pockets and My Girlfriend's Hungry, Blues," and sang it on his guitar while I drove the sulking girls home. The next weekend they wouldn't go with us.

"Maybe they didn't like your singing, Huck," I said.

He punched me on the arm to show me he wasn't offended and laughed. "The heck with those Flute-snoots." Huck called stuck-up people Flute-snoots. "Let's go to the Crown dance instead. Lot's of girls up there, and they're not too stuck-up to dance with us."

We paid our fifty cents admission and strolled into the crowded hall in the middle of a set. I stared, my mouth hanging open, as guys in short sleeved shirts and girls in bright dresses whirled and twirled to the singsong orders of the Caller.

"Do-si-do your partner, now your corner. Al-a-monde left. Swing!"

Skirts flared out showing rows of white lacy petticoats. Guys skipped and leaped around and grabbed girls and laid hands on their waists and shoulders and swung them around. Some girls lost their footing and were whirled straight out, feet above the dance floor, until they were red in the face and laughing. Above all these goings on, the accordion, and fiddle and two guitars filled the hall with boot-stomping music.

Huck found a partner for the next dance by asking the first girl he spotted sitting along the wall. I hung back, still stinging from the rejection of the girl from Marble. Mostly, I was afraid to make a fool of myself on the dance floor. I sat down on the edge of the stage with the girlfriends of the musicians and the other guys too shy to dance. We all sat and listened to the calls while watching the others dance.

It took me more than a month, going to the dances every Saturday night and watching from the stage, before I learned every dance by heart. Huck went through several girl friends before I finally worked up enough courage to get up and dance. As it turned out, the girl asked me.

It was a thin crowd that night at Crown. One of the sets lacked a fourth couple. No one remained on the sidelines to get up and dance. Betty Hepfl, the girlfriend of Ed Wolbert, the accordion player, slid off the edge of the stage and grabbed my arm.

"Come on, Dave! They need one more couple or the dance won't go on. We're it. There isn't anyone else."

I hung back, eyeballing big Ed. I knew he had a jealous streak. I surely didn't want to make trouble. Ed scowled over the keys and buttons of his instrument. He stared me up and down, at my farmer boy clothes and Sunday shoes polished to hide the scuffs.

"Come on, Ed," Betty pleaded. "He's just a kid."

Finally Ed nodded. "OK Dave. But no funny stuff, you hear? I don't take kindly to any smart aleck who tries to swing my girl off her feet."

I glanced at Betty, a solid farm girl with sun-browned, well-muscled arms from pitching hay. Even though I had been hefting sixty-pound sacks of grain since I turned twelve, I doubted I could swing Betty off her feet.

"Don't worry, Ed. Your girl's safe with me."

The music began. We danced. As soon as we started the first al-a-monde left, I knew I was in big trouble. My Sunday shoes with their slippery leather soles threatened to put me butt over tin cup on the very first turn. Before I could warn Betty, she grabbed me and whirled me into a lusty swing. Down we went in a heap in the middle of the dance floor. Betty went down first. I landed on top of her.

The music stopped.

I braced myself for a good thrashing that would surely come as soon as Ed had time to shuck off his accordion. I scrambled to my feet and helped Betty up. We turned toward the stage expecting the worse. The musicians, their instruments stilled, stared at Betty and me. Their faces, those stern Wolbert faces, got redder and redder. Suddenly they all broke up. Laughter exploded over the microphone. The fiddle player beckoned me closer.

"Here kid, put some rosin on those leather soles before you kill somebody."

The dance went on. After that, I learned to wear my knobby-soled work shoes to the dances. Safer that way.

* * *

Cecile

Square dancing had always been a favorite activity of my parents. As young girls, Mother and her sisters used to walk to the Crown dances from their North Pine Grove home. They thought nothing of the four-mile walk there and back. Pretty and popular, the Black girls— Elva, Loretta and Ruth—danced every set. Their youngest sister, Gertie, a toddler at that time, stayed home with Ma and Pa. One Saturday afternoon, Loretta, fooling around with the bread knife in the kitchen, accidentally slashed open a long cut on Ruth's buttocks. The sisters taped Ruth together and all three went to Crown dance that evening with the strong warning to Ruth not to laugh too much or she'd rip apart.

Pop, a dancing fool since early youth, learned the steps and calls by dancing at house parties and the Grange Hall at *Shigawake*, Quebec. Pop taught each of his daughters to dance, taking us out on the dance floor when we were as young as eleven. When my oldest sister Joy got married, I danced every set with relatives and my parents' card playing buddies. So when Mother and Pop decided to attend the Crown dance during Pop's annual July vacation in 1950, I went along.

It capped a week of changes for me. I graduated from St. Paul's on Sunday, June 25, 1950. There would be a new school for me in September. I wasn't sure how I felt about attending public high school. Most of my girl friends would attend Mount St. Mary's, but my parents frowned on the high tuition costs for a private girls' school, $250 a year!

Then, when we went down to Pennsylvania, more changes awaited me. My cousin, Jimmy Baumcratz, and I, for the first time in our short lives, would not be allowed to share the company cot on the back porch as we had since babyhood.

"You're too old now," Aunt Gertie insisted. I turned fourteen that spring; Jimmy was thirteen. Neither Gertie nor Mother would explain further.

Jimmy and I were puzzled by being separated. We wondered why parents made up such silly rules. We vowed to spend as much time together during the day to make up for the long giggling conversations and word games we used to enjoy at night in our shared cot. So when Mother and Pop left to visit Aunt Ruth, I stayed behind to play baseball with Jimmy, his cousins Mary and John, and a few of the Snyder boys.

* * *

David

"I tell you, Dave, the girls around here are all Flute-snoots."

Huck and I were bellied up to the bar at Gust Wolbert's Beer

Garden in Snydersburg. We were drinking Iron City draft and complaining about our love lives, or actually, the lack of love in our lives. "Ain't that right, Gustie?"

Behind the bar, Gust just grinned. He'd heard it all before, I guess. I fished out another quarter and pointed toward our empty glasses.

Huck took a long slurp of his beer and sighed. "So are we going to the Crown dance tonight, or what?"

I shifted on the bar stool and stared glumly into the foaming glass in my hand. "What's the use of going to the dance?"

"Well, you dance, don't you?"

"Yeah. But afterwards, when I try for a date, all the girls turn me down."

"Flute-snoots."

"Yeah. They think they're too good for a farmer's son like me."

Huck twirled around on his stool a couple of times. Just watching him made me dizzy. When he slid to his feet, he staggered. "Come on, Dave. Let's go home. Uncle Cecil and Aunt Elvie are coming over this afternoon."

"Who?"

"My aunt and uncle from New York."

Huck stood there, weaving slightly as he lit a cigarette. I followed him outside to the Chevy parked nose first at the edge of the tavern steps. Huck climbed in the driver's seat and slammed the door. I hurried over to the other side. Sometimes Huck forgot I was along and took off before I got in the passenger door. Not this day. Huck sat quietly, frowning through the fog of cigarette smoke trailing from the edge of his lips. I turned to see what he was looking at, but all I saw was the mud splatters on the windshield.

"I've got a girl for you, Dave!" he said and bounced up and down on the seat.

I just looked at him, wondering if this was another of his jokes.

"No, Dave. Honest!"

"What kind of girl?" I asked, immediately suspicious. "Another girl like those gold diggers from Marble?"

"No! A nice girl. My cousin, Cecile. Elvie's youngest daughter."

I sat for a minute, trying to remember. "You mean that skinny kid, kind of serious? The baseball player? Too *young*!"

"Give her a chance, boy. You're not exactly ready for the old rocking chair, you know, even if tomorrow is your birthday. *Sweet nineteen and never been kissed,*" he mocked in a high girlish voice. He puckered up his freckled face and made disgusting kissing noises with his mouth. We wrestled on the front seat until Huck yelled *Uncle*! Then we broke apart laughing.

Huck started up the car by grinding down on the round starter button with his foot. He played with the clutch while stirring the floor shifting stick. *Clun*k! It slipped into reverse and roared backwards onto the muddy road.

"Sure will be glad when they get this road paved again," Huck said.

His cigarette bobbled up and down while he talked. Now in the middle of the road, he fought again with the shift lever.

"We're going to have to fix this tranny one of these days," he said.

Clunk! We roared through Snydersburg in first gear. Huck kept crooning some dumb song about a corker of a New Yorker, and giving me rolly-eyed looks, until I threatened to punch him a good one. Just past Och's Lumber Mill, Huck skipped second gear and shoved the stick directly into third. *Clunk!*

"Ahh!" he said, satisfied.

As he turned to sing some other dumb song, his cigarette dropped out of his mouth. I dove to the floor, searching for the hot butt. Before I knew it, Huck was down there helping me hunt for it too.

"Wait a minute! Who's driving?"

Just then the car tilted, shuddered and stopped. We were in the ditch, and no amount of pushing or wheel spinning would heave the car out. Huck laughed. "Well, guess we'd better walk the rest of the way," he said.

Walk we did, weaving, stumbling, sometimes singing and punching, all the way to Jack Bauer's driveway. Huck's father, sitting on the porch talking to Elva and Cecil Ramier, jumped down and hurried out to meet us.

"Where's your car, Huck?" Jack demanded.

"In the ditch!" Huck laughed.

"You dumb fool, you're drunk!"

"Listen Mack," Huck said boldly, "it's my car. I'll drive it in the ditch if I feel like it."

Jack reared back one big fist. "I'll 'Mack' you!"

Cecil, who had followed Jack out, stood listening with his hands in his pockets. When Jack cocked his fist, Cecil took both hands out of his pockets and grabbed Jack's arm.

"Don't hit the kid, Jack," he said.

To everyone's surprise, Jack dropped his fist and turned away. "Just don't expect any help from me, Huck," he said and walked away.

We started down to Art Bauer's, Huck's uncle, to get one of the boys to bring up a tractor. As we staggered past Jack's front yard, I craned my neck looking for a skinny girl with dark hair who might be playing baseball out back. All eight of Huck's brothers and sisters sat lined up on the edge of the porch, calling out insults as we stumbled past. No little cousin sat among them.

Just my luck. I'd never get a girl.

* * *

Cecile

I didn't know whether to go to Crown dance or not. Jimmy wouldn't be going. He had to babysit his sister, Joan, and my little brother, Jimbo. Maybe I should stay home too?

"Come on, Kiddo," Pop insisted, "it will be fun."

Aunt Gertie and Uncle Fritz primped at the kitchen mirror over the sink. Mother's feet sounded from above as she trotted to and fro getting dressed. Pop waited at the table, smoking, and whistling through his teeth. I hurried upstairs and changed into my blue circle skirt and white peter pan blouse. I hooked together my black cinch belt and tied a red silk scarf at my throat. On my feet I wore penny loafers and white ankle socks. I glanced into the distorted mirror over the dresser as I smoothed my pageboy hairdo. A teenage fashion maven of the 1950's.

"I'm ready," I said.

Already the excitement of the coming dance filled me with shivers of anticipation. Jimmy, Joan and Jimbo, stared forlornly as they waved from the back door.

"We're going to Crown to the dance!" Mother said. Her voice swelled with the memory of past good times.

Pop and Fritz sat up front. Gertie, Mother and I held down the back. That's how it always has been in Pennsylvania: men in the front, women in the back seat. Gertie started to sing, "Rose of San Antonio." I joined in. We sang all the way to Crown

As we approached St. Mary's Church, the road narrowed and turned back on itself. Overhead, heavy leafy branches dipped down and brushed the top of the Plymouth. Fritz and Pop argued baseball: Bisons against the Pirates. In the back seat, silence fell as Mother and Gertie relived their shared past. Mother turned her head to stare at the familiar brick hulk of St. Mary's Church. Its steeple looked tall and white against the darkening sky. Her grandparents, the Blacks and Dobsons, immigrants from Ireland, were buried in the churchyard. Her parents, all her siblings, and Mother, had been Baptized, received First Communion and Confirmation and exchanged vows of Matrimony all in the same little country church at Crown. Her parents, Mary and Charles Black, along with Edward a younger brother, were buried in a triple grave under the shared headstone Mother bought with money saved from Pop's salary at Dunlap Tire and Rubber.

As we drove past the churchyard cemetery, Aunt Gertie grew pale and still. She glanced once up the hill to the familiar gravesite, then looked away. Gertie had been five when her mother died of untreated diabetes (no insulin then), a year older when her brother died. She was barely twelve when her Pa was killed by the bull.

They lived alone, Charles Black and his youngest daughter. She walked each day to the schoolhouse while Pa ran the farm. When she returned from school that afternoon, she found the house empty. Later, her uncle found the body and shot the bull. No one ever talked about that terrible time.

Years later, a few days before she died, my mother finally told me about the death of her father. Gertie never spoke of it at all. I understand now the reasons for my aunt's stringent rules enforced on her children, the unbendable insistence that she know where her loved ones were every minute of every day. How else could she feel safe? I didn't understand her vigilance then. I only sensed that brief moment of tenseness as she stared up the hill to her parents' grave, her face pale and drawn in the shadows of the back seat. The moment passed. Gertie turned her eyes toward the dance hall ahead and started another song.

* * *

David

It took Huck and me all afternoon to fix his car. It hadn't been damaged when it ran into the ditch, but the transmission definitely needed adjusting. We were sprawled under the car, wrenches in hands, busting our knuckles over two stubborn bolts, when someone stepped on my foot.

"Cut it out!" I yelled. Thinking Huck's sister Louise was playing a trick, I cut loose with a string of German cuss words learned from Dad.

"Oh, excuse me." A smiling face topped by wavy gray hair peeked under the running board. "I thought you were Charles."

"Aunt Elvie! Are you trying to cripple my buddy?" Huck asked. "We want to go to the dance tonight, you know." He pretended to be mad.

Aunt Elvie blushed and walked away.

"Better watch out, Dave," Huck said. "She might be your mother-in-law someday."

"Ah, button your lip, Huck."

"You want me to cut off your head and throw it in your face?"

It's a wonder we ever got any work done with Huck and his corny jokes.

* * *

Cecile

The dance hall was full. People of all ages ... gray haired couples, the men in shirt sleeves and vests, the women in silk dresses, teenagers in carefully pressed slacks and skirts topped by short sleeved cotton shirts, youngsters in their Sunday best ... all crowded around the dance floor and lined up around the walls on wooden benches. Up on stage, the Wolbert brothers tuned up their instruments. A nod from the Caller and the fiddlers stirred up a lively tune. On the dance floor, couples formed sets of eight people, four pair of men and women who faced each other in a set pattern. The Head Couple, the pair with their backs to the Caller, led off the action.

"Head couple, promenade the outside,
Now the inside, now the outside.

Join hands, couple in the center,
And swing your little darlin' if you dare."

Mother and Dad, Gertie and Fritz, joined a square immediately. I found a seat on the bench to watch. After three or four different songs, the squares broke up and the musicians played waltzes and polkas. When the accordion player shouted, "Form your sets, square up!" Pop led me out for a dance. Caught up with the heel stomping, skirt flying music, I grinned all the way through the set.

* * *

David

Huck and I stood at the back of the dance floor watching the action.

"There! See? There she is!" Huck poked me with his elbow and pointed.

I stared across the sea of bobbing heads, the upraised elbows as the men twirled the girls. Huck was right; his little cousin had grown up. I watched her face. No longer wearing the serious frown of a dedicated baseball player, she looked flushed and glowing as she passed from hand to hand, from man to man, swinging out her skirt and stomping her feet to the beat of the music. She wasn't flirting with the guys in her set, and I liked that. She seemed more interested in listening to the Caller's instructions. She waited, eyes down, head tilted to hear the next call. Dark slightly wavy hair brushed her shoulders. She looked up once and her big brown eyes seemed to stare right into mine. Something in my chest started hopping around like a flea in a mitten. Then the music carried her away again. I fought my way outside and stood around with the yahoos who were drinking sloe gin and beer. Huck took me aside.

"What's the matter? Aren't you going to ask her to dance?"

I shook my head.

"Why not?"

"She won't dance with me."

"What? Are you crazy? Sure she will."

"She's a city girl." I just stood there feeling like a dumb, tongue-tied farm boy. "She will never dance with me. Never."

"She may be a city girl, Dave, but she's got a country heart."

I shrugged, huddled up in misery. Huck sighed.

"Dave, I'm gonna prove something right now."

"What?"

I didn't want to talk. I wanted to go off somewhere and dream about a young dark eyed city girl who wouldn't even know I thought about her. Huck grabbed my arm and shook me.

"Come on! We're going back in there. I'm gonna prove that Cecile will dance with you."

"Sure. How?"

Huck jabbed his thumb into his chest. "I'm going to ask her to dance. If she'll dance with me, she will dance with anybody. Right?"

"Well...I don't know."

We went back inside.

* * *

Cecile

Huck's sister Louise and I sat together on the wallflower's bench. I hadn't danced again after that one dance with Pop.

"It's your own fault, Kiddo," Pop insisted. "If you had said yes to that first boy who asked you, you would have danced every set."

"Louise turned him down first," I protested.

Louise fussed with her pretty red hair. "I never liked that boy," she said. "He used to pull my hair in school." She glanced at me and grinned. "But you could have danced with him, Celie."

"Now you tell me!"

We giggled together.

"Form your sets!" the Caller announced.

Couples leaped to their feet. A hurried scramble among the wallflower's bench emptied the bench except for Louise and me. We both looked up as Huck approached.

"I ain't gonna dance with you, Huck. So don't ask," Louise said.

"Don't want to dance with you, Flute-snoot," he said. "How about you, Cousin?"

I leaped up and grabbed his offered arm. We skipped out on the dance floor and kicked up our heels. I wondered why the cousin I always called Charles had suddenly wanted to dance with me. He hadn't paid much attention to me since he used to pluck me out of his mother's pea patch when I was a toddler and he a mature ten-year-old. It surprised me to notice we were now the same height. I could feel his bony ribs as we swung. The hardened strength in his callused hands left me breathless as we twirled around.

During the square, when we had changed partners according to the Caller's instructions, my temporary partner, Pete Shill, asked me for the following dance. I nodded, happy and bewildered by my sudden popularity. It was simple country logic, I learned later. At dances, where everyone knows everyone else, newcomers are watched to see if they are there to dance or to sit out the sets. When I turned down the first boy, I was immediately judged a non-dancer by every unattached male in the hall. Dancing with Pop didn't count. Fathers always danced with their daughters at least once. But when I stepped out with Charles, the signals changed. Suddenly I was available, an unattached female willing to dance.

The Caller announced, "Promenade her to the old rocking chair." The square broke up.

Charles took my elbow and steered me to the back of the hall. "I want you to meet a friend of mine," he said.

* * *

David

I stood at the back of the hall and watched Huck dance with his cousin. The longer I watched, the more miserable I felt. It should have been me out there twirling her around, touching her hands, putting my arm around her waist, laughing into her eyes. Instead, my friend had all the fun while I hung back too shy to open my trap.

Suddenly the music ended. Huck and his cousin were heading straight for me! I wanted to run but my shoes seemed glued to the floor. All around me guys were shoving at each other, cracking jokes, heading outside for a quick nip or a slug of beer. I stood rooted to the floor, watching as Huck carefully steered his little cousin through the crowd. Then they were right in front of me. She was close enough to reach out and touch. I swallowed down a hard lump in my throat and tried to think of something to say.

"Dave, this is the girl I told you about."

I stared. I could feel my face get hot. I nodded.

Huck sighed. He turned to his cousin. "Cecile, this big dummy is my best friend, Dave."

She smiled. Her face, flushed by the dance, grew redder as she stared at her feet. She said nothing. Huck looked from one of us to the other. His eyes rolled as he realized his matchmaker chores hadn't ended yet.

"Dave? Didn't you want to ask her something?"

My mouth opened, finally, maybe from the poke Huck gave me in the ribs.

"Uhhh ..."

She lifted her head and opened those pretty brown eyes wider. She smiled.

"Would you dance with me next?" The words came all in a rush. Oh heck! I said it all wrong. She'd think I wanted to round dance, and I didn't know a waltz from a polka. Panic thickened my tongue. "I mean, can I have the next square ..." My throat filled. I had to swallow hard before I could finish, "... with you, I mean."

A little frown puckered the space between her eyebrows. Even before she spoke, I knew she would turn me down. I messed up my chance. Now I'd never get to know her. The nicest girl I ever saw. And I lost her before I even had a chance to know her.

* * *

Cecile

He was the handsomest boy I ever saw. He had big brown eyes and wavy hair. One stubborn lock of hair fell over his forehead. He kept brushing it back with one blunt-fingered hand. I wanted to reach up and help brush it back. His muscular shoulders and well-developed arms looked perfect for swinging a girl off her feet. It would have been heaven to dance with him. But I had promised the last dance to Pete Shill!

"I'm sorry," I said. The way his face changed from eager hopefulness to acute misery told me I had hurt him. "I would love to dance with you, but I already promised someone else."

He turned away and pushed through the crowd around the door. I had lost him. I'd never see him again. Oh, if only there had been one more dance! If only Pete Shill hadn't asked me first. If only I hadn't promised ... But it was too late for if only. I would never see Dave again.

* * *

David

I missed my chance by standing there like a dummy instead of asking her right off. Now it was too late. I'd never get another chance to dance with Cecile. I'd never see her again.

***

David and Cecile

But God had other plans for us. Two years later, after exchanging a trunk full of love letters, we were wed. Thanks Huck.

Cherish Every Moment.

CHAPTER 3

⚜

That Memorable First Kiss

That summer after Dave and I met at the Crown dance, nudged by my matchmaker cousin Huck, we began exchanging letters. What a thrill to reach into the mailbox on my parents' house and fetch a hand-written letter from a boy! I examined the envelope, savoring each little detail. The stamp (a three cent stamp in those good old days)was affixed upside down. *Hmmm, wonder what that means?* A careless person's last minute slap dash way of gluing stamps onto an envelope? Or maybe something else, something more romantic! Being just fourteen years old, every small detail of my very first love letter throbbed with importance. The upside down stamp just had to be *romantic!* Musing, my heart already beating fast with anticipation, I flipped the envelope over to open it. Scrawled across the flap of the envelope, in red ink, *S.W.A.K.*

"Swak? What the heck is that?" I muttered and thumbed open the letter.

Later, I would discover the meaning behind the postal code. The upside down stamp meant *I miss you,* the swak, meant *Sealed*

With A Kiss. But that morning, scanning the letter as I hurried off to a Girl Scout meeting nearby, each word within the body of the letter skipped my heart.

> *Dear Cele (he didn't know how to spell my name, yet),*
> *How are you? I am fine. I am sorry we did not get to dance*
> *at Crown. I wanted to ask you all evening, but couldn't*
> *work up the nerve. Will your family be coming down for*
> *Labor Day? There is a dance at Fryburg then, and we*
> *could go together, I hope? I have been putting on a new*
> *barn roof for my Dad. Hope I don't fall off because I really*
> *want to see you again. Yours, Dave.*

At the bottom of the page, a drawn heart and another puzzling lovers' code: S.W.A.K.

I returned his letter that week and our twice-a-week letters flew back and forth from state to state. By the middle of August, we were eagerly awaiting the Fryburg dance and our first date together. Then tragedy struck. One of my father's sisters died, Aunt Blanche. Pop took the train up to Quebec to attend her funeral. Mother didn't drive, and I, of course, was too young to drive.

"My life is over!" I wept to my older sister, Betty. "My first date with the nicest guy in the world and now we can't even go!"

Betty, bless her romantic soul, volunteered to drive Dad's 1940 Plymouth so Mother, little brother, Jimbo, and me could go to Pennsylvania for the Labor Day weekend. This was a real sacrifice on Betty's part. She had married out of the church several years before. Our relatives in Pennsylvania were died-in-the-wool Catholics. When a girl married out of the church, she was shunned, much like the Amish do in today's world. Betty suffered in silence as our aunts and uncles ignored her completely. Caught up in the excitement of my first date, I did not realize how my loving middle sister was hurt by the rude actions of our relatives. Even though she was treated like a leper, Betty still kept up a smiling front for me, her little sister, as we both got ready for the big dance at Fryburg. She fussed over my hair, dabbed a bit of cream perfume behind my ears, and even applied my lipstick.

"You look wonderful, little Sis," she said. "You actually glow!"

Betty of course, looked gorgeous. A knock-em-dead vivacious blonde, she wore a sleeveless sun dress that complimented her golden tan. When we arrived at the dance, Betty was mobbed by old friends from her teen years, and a few new guys in the crowd, visitors from Ohio or Pittsburgh. Each admiring man wanted a dance with Betty. A few even gave me a look-over and offered to step out on the dance floor with me. Beside me, Dave's glowering stare changed their minds.

"She's with me!" he growled.

Both sisters danced every dance. Betty whirled with a different dance partner each time. I stuck like a happy glue to my soon to be life-partner, Dave. We were all sorry when the dance ended. In exhausted silence we filed out to the car. Uncle Fritz, Aunt Gertie, and Mother sat in the front. Betty, Dave and me, took up the back, with me in the middle. He held my hand on the too short trip back to Snydersburg, where we were staying. Betty hummed a little song. The adults up front seemed too tired to talk. When Fritz spoke, we all jumped.

"Where do you want to be dropped off, young man?" he said gruffly over his shoulder.

"At Jack's will be fine, thanks," Dave said. He had no car at that time and would have to walk two miles home, in the dark of night, from Uncle Jack's house.

As Fritz pulled into Jack's driveway, Dave leaned forward and turned toward me.

"I really enjoyed the dance," he said, his voice low and intimate.

"Me too," I said.

Mother and Aunt Gertie climbed out of the front seat and folded back the seat so Dave could get out. Dave leaned toward me to give me a kiss, our first kiss. I turned toward him and placed my sandaled foot on the crease of the folded seat as our lips touched briefly.

Every girl of my generation dreamed about her first kiss. Raised on fairy tales of Sleeping Beauty and Cinderella, we fantasized about a Prince Charming who would give us a kiss so swooningly wonderful that it would knock our socks off, or leave behind a glass slipper as a reminder of that special event.

Our first kiss was something like that. Only thing, while we young lovers gently touched lips, Mother let go of the folded front seat to talk to Gertie, and it flopped back on my bare toes. Gave them a pretty good pinch, too. I limped for days after.

Was that first kiss worth it? You betcha!

Cherish Every Moment.

CHAPTER 4

❦

Dating Mishaps:
the Good Night Echo

Two years after we met at the Crown dance, Dave moved up to the Buffalo area to be near me. He found a job working for Sports-Service, a Concession company. He moved into a rooming house nearby, within walking distance of my home in Kenmore. After the old 1940 Plymouth he owned died, we were car-less, so we did a lot of walking. But that was a normal way of life back in the early 1950's. Teens seldom had their own wheels, unless you counted bicycles. After working a full day in Buffalo, Dave took a bus to his rooming house, cleaned up, and went to a nearby diner to eat.

I also had a job, as a part time clerk working three evenings a week for Woolworth's (a variety store commonly called a Five-and-Dime store). I worked at the Notions' counter from after school until the store closed at 9 p.m. On nights when I worked, Dave rode the Delaware Avenue bus to the Sheridan Plaza and waited for me to finish my shift. In rainy weather, we sometimes rode the bus back to a stop about a mile from my house. But most of the time, we walked the two or three miles home, so that we could spend a little more time together. Not only that, the bus fare we saved went toward our future life together as man and wife. I already wore his engagement ring. We were making plans for our future.

Sometimes on weekends, we spent the evening at home, watching the tiny television set in my parents' living room. The black and white images flickering across the twelve inch screen were the latest thing in modern entertainment. *Uncle Miltie*, or *Show of Shows*, the *Ed Sullivan Show* on Sunday night. Nothing much else on all week, so we walked to the local movie theater for the evening show. After the movies were over (they showed two full length movies each night, plus a newsreel and a cartoon between them), Dave always walked me home. Even in those days of comparative personal safety, young women did not walk the streets after dark. Not if she had a loving boyfriend like mine, anyway!

One evening, we lingered over our farewells in the back hall of my parents' home, trying to be quiet and not wake up the folks. The kisses were getting longer and more serious those days. We were deeply in love, I wore his tiny engagement ring with pride. Another year and I would be out of school and ready for the life-long commitment of marriage. In the meantime, parting was such sweet sorrow, or so the movie heroines claimed.

One Sunday night, he seemed to be in a hurry to say goodnight. *Is he losing interest in me?* I wondered. *Is all the walking making him too tired to even give me a nice kiss good night?*

"One more kiss and I have to go," Dave whispered. "'Cheer up, boys, work tomorrow'," he said quoting my father. "And you have to get up early for school."

Uncertain about his feelings for me, yet overcome with deep affection for my farm boy, I reached around him and gave him a tremendous, rib-cracking hug.

"Barummmmmp!"

A long, noisy fart rattled around the confines of the small hallway.

To say I was astonished was the understatement of the year. No one in our inhibited family ever released intestinal gas in public! It just wasn't done in polite society, especially in mixed company, at least not then in the early 1950's.

Now of course, passing gas is as common as cell phones and DVD players. But that evening, Dave's indiscretion created a sensation. It echoed around the small hallway. The noxious fumes stung our eyes.

Dave blushed bright red. "So sorry! I tried to hold it until I got outside."

He look mortified. I laughed so hard I choked, all while striving and failing to be quiet.

From my parents' bedroom, a sleepy voice said sternly, "Time to break it up, Kids."

We laughed harder, all while struggling to be quiet. My sides hurt, and his did too, I imagine, from the fierce hug

Giggling and sputtering with barely contained hysteria, we stumbled out into the driveway that separated my parents' house from our neighbors, the Shields. Dave's noisy indiscretion must have startled Mr. Shields too, because his bedroom window went up and he leaned out.

"Everything all right, you two?" he asked.

Dave answered with another long, uncontrollable fart.

"Sorry," he said, choking on his words. "Beans for supper."

The window slammed down. Even through the closed window, we could hear Mr. Shields' laughter.

Fifty-five years later, Dave no longer tries to suppress his intestinal gas. In fact, every time I make a suggestion that he dislikes, he answers with a long whining fart. But then, we have been married more than a half century, through thick and thin, good times and bad times, sickness and health. An occasional fart is overlooked. Why sweat the small stuff?

Cherish Every Moment.

CHAPTER 5

༺❀༻

Evening in Paris

Back when Dave and I were dating, his very first gift to me was a lovely blue bottle of *Evening in Paris* perfume. Available in any drugstore at that time, this scent seemed to be the most popular smell-good product around. If a beau gave a gal a bottle of *Evening in Paris*, things were getting pretty serious indeed. Even the name invoked romantic visions of a faraway city, languid evenings where lovers walked arm in arm beneath a low hanging French moon.

The gift made me feel special, a mature teenager with French-Canadian roots and *real* French perfume. Sometimes, to make my school friends jealous, I would dab a tiny smidgen behind each ear and wear it to swim class. My girlfriend Joanne, whom I had known since third grade at St. Paul's, would grin and snort.

"Why waste that expensive perfume wearing it to school?" she said. "It's *Evening in Paris,* right? Save it for special evenings."

Somehow, wearing it for an evening spent with Dave at the local movie house watching "Bride of Frankenstein" did not seem all that a special an occasion. So the pretty blue bottle stayed mostly full until we were married in November, 1952.

Our wedding date fell just before Thanksgiving. We skipped the honeymoon trip and moved right into our very own apartment in the Black Rock section of Buffalo. We lived in the upper rear of a four apartment building. I kept busy doing housewifely things while Dave walked to work at Sports-Service Inc. on Ferry Street. We had no car at that time, couldn't afford it. The rent took up half of Dave's salary of $45 a week. On payday, twice a month, we took the bus downtown to see a movie. On those rare occasions, I wore my special perfume. Life was good. We might be dirt poor, yet the bottle of *Evening in Paris* never failed to make me feel rich and very French.

The day before Christmas that year, I was busy making Christmas cookies. Mother, Pop, and kid brother Jimbo, were expected over for the evening. I hummed as I baked. All of the cookies came out black on the bottom (the oven in the old range baked 100-degrees hotter than the gauge, but what did I know?). I kept busy scraping each batch of cookies to color, hoping the icing would hide their scorched flavor. The doorbell rang. Expecting Joanne, who had promised to come over that day, I stood at the top of the steps and hollered down.

"Come on up, the door is open."

The lower door opened on a strange sight. Two beefy men on either side of Dave supported a very wobbly husband. The men looked warily at the spatula in my hand. Would I fling it down on them?

"What happened?" I said, afraid that Dave had an accident at work.

"Too much Christmas party," one man said.

"Oh, I didn't know Dave was a drinking man," I said, "Bring him up."

The other man grinned. "Apparently, Dave is *not* a drinking man."

They hauled Dave up the steps, knocking against the walls on either side as the three of them swayed from side to side. The heavy sweet smell of whiskey fumes filled the narrow hallway. As they muscled Dave past me toward the bedroom, I pointed to the bed and they flung him across it. He gave one long groan and passed out.

The guy nearest the door apologized as the other one trotted down the steps.

"We're sorry, Mrs. Bauer. We had a drinking game and the kid won. Or lost, take your pick."

He, too, departed quickly. Maybe they had Christmas parties in other years and angry wives had chased them, waving spatulas? Whatever. I looked in on Dave. Out for the count. He even slept through supper, a rare occasion. Farm boys never miss supper!

That evening, as I got dressed up a little bit for my parents' visit, Dave still sprawled across the bed. He had not vomited, nor had he eaten anything. He did apologize.

"Never again," he promised. "Never!"

I combed my hair and hid a grin. Nothing like a miserable drinking experience to stop a would-be problem in its tracks. As I dabbed a bit of perfume behind each ear, Dave groaned loudly.

"What is that horrible smell?"

I laughed out loud. "Why it's that special perfume you gave me last year, *Evening in Paris*."

"I think I am going to be sick!"

Needless to say, Dave did not ever get drunk on whiskey again in all the fifty plus years we have been married. I didn't use that special perfume anymore either.

Cherish Every Moment.

❧❀❧

CHAPTER 6

The Miracle of Birth

David
Tuesday, July 14, 1953

A sharp elbow hit me in the ribs. I jerked awake. Beside me, Cecile rolled to the edge of the bed, her belly huge with the child who would soon be our firstborn.

"What? Is it time?"

She sat up slowly, hugging her pain tight. She nodded.

I leaped out of bed, scared and confused.

"What do I do now? Call the taxi? Get dressed? What should I wear?"

I mean after all, what *did* a soon-to-be-father wear to the hospital? This was a special occasion. Even I knew enough not to wear my work uniform with the *Sport-service* label on the shirt pocket.

"Should I wear the new suit I wore to our wedding? How about a white shirt, tie and my dress pants?"

"You mean your gravy pants?" She called them my gravy pants because every time I wore them out to dinner, I always managed to spill gravy on them.

Even to my own ears, my scattered words sounded like the babble of a kid trying to escape the strap. She touched my arm and giggled, tickled by my silly concern of what to wear to our birthing party. We had been ready for two weeks now. The suitcase sat by the door. The crib and bassinet, blankets folded neatly, waited in the bedroom of our third floor flat in North Buffalo. We were ready. At least I *hoped* we were ready! Right now I felt pretty scared and not ready at all.

"Smile, Daddy," she said, "today you become a father."

She got dressed slowly, stopping every few minutes to bend over and gasp. I threw on the clothes she pointed at, a yellow short-sleeved pullover shirt and my everyday pants. Then I hurried to the living room and called a taxi. We waited just inside the main doorway, at the bottom of the stairway, down three flights of steps. I held her as she leaned against me, sometimes gasping with pain. When the cab driver arrived, and caught sight of my wife, huge with child, his eyes bugged out. It looked comical, the fright shining on his face in a thin sheet of nervous sweat. I hoped he wouldn't bolt like a nervous horse. No, he might be scared, but he was man enough to do his duty.

"Which hospital?"

"Children's Hospital, on Elmwood."

He nodded, "I know where it is."

He took the suitcase from me and tossed it in his front seat. We climbed in back for the short eight-block ride. On a better day, we could have walked, it was less than a mile, but not today.

As we rocketed like a bat out of hell down Delaware Avenue in the middle of that hot summer's night, the driver ran a couple of red lights. I had the feeling that if he had a siren, it would have been screaming. One time a big pothole showed up in the middle of the Utica Street intersection. He jammed on the brakes, swerved to the right, then the left, and we almost rolled off the back seat. No seat belts then, of course. Just hang on and pray through that wild ride.

"Sorry," the cabby said. His eyes rolled and showed a lot of white in the rearview mirror.

Finally we arrived at the hospital. I helped Cecile climb out of the taxi. She stood weaving and moaning. I fumbled in my pocket for my wallet to pay the driver. Then, even before I managed to dig out some loose change for a tip, he sped away.

Once inside, Cecile was whisked off to the Maternity floor while I got stuck with the paper work. We didn't have insurance then, so I signed a paper that promised to pay the bill. I knew my wife had been saving money for months to cover the hospital bill, so that part didn't worry me none. I just wanted to be with her now, and forget about anything else.

Giving birth in those days was a lot different than it is now. Fathers were not allowed in the delivery room. In fact, a father-to-be was lucky to see his wife at all once the nurses took her away! A nice woman in a pink striped uniform directed me toward the elevator. I rode up two floors and sat in the waiting room until a nurse came and got me.

Cecile sat on the edge of a hospital bed in a white gown, open at the back. Her private parts *down there* had been shaved. She had also been given an enema, "To make delivery easier," the nurse explained. So in between pains, about every five minutes, my wife would trot off to a nearby bathroom. At first she would struggle into a robe. Toward the last, she just trotted off without the robe, letting the whole world see her bottom hanging out the back of that white hospital gown! It shocked me, that lack of modesty in my really private wife. But I guess she just got fed up with the chore of flinging on the robe.

What happened next shocked me even more. As her labor pains got harder, and closer together, she started to yell and holler.

I never heard her yell before, never. She had always been so soft spoken. I had to lean close to hear her voice sometimes. Now she was screaming like a wild animal with her tail caught in a trap. It was embarrassing! During one particularly long howl, I reached across the bed and put my hand on her mouth to muffle the screams.

She bit me!

I leaped back, examining my hand for blood. It only showed a couple of teeth marks. Whew, blood makes me weak in the knees. Ever since a horseshoe nail took a hunk out of my leg, the sight of blood makes we woozy. The nurse came in then, with a long needle contraption in her hand.

"Time to take the edge off, huh Mama?"

Cecile nodded, swiping at tears on her cheeks. The nurse gave me a glare.

"Time for you to go out in the waiting room, Sir. We will let you know when the baby is born."

I beat a hasty retreat. I waited. No other father waited in that lonely room. Just me and my suddenly guilty conscience. *Now why did I try to quiet her screams, just when things were getting really rough for her? What kind of man treats his wife like that?*

"But she didn't have to bite me, either," I mumbled and rubbed my sore hand. *Next time, she can just go through her labor alone if she's gonna act like a wildcat ... If there is a next time,* I thought grimly.

It seemed like a lifetime before anyone came to talk to me again. Felt like I was being punished, to tell the truth. My eyes started getting heavy. All the rough stuff we had both been through in the past few hours wore me out ... the wild cab ride, the worry, the sight of my usually silent wife screaming, the scene at her bedside when she bit me, the lack of sleep... caught up with me. I must have been snoring because the nurse who shook me awake was grinning fit to kill.

"Wake up, Daddy. You have a son."

I leaped to my feet, heart pounding like a flea in a mitten.

"What? A son, you say?" I couldn't stop grinning. A son! *A son!*

"Where is he? I want to see him. Is my wife OK?" The questions tumbled out of me. I was babbling like a dang fool. But my heart just kept hammering. *A son!*

"Little Mama is doing fine. Come see your son."

The nurse herded me toward the nursery window. I peered through the glass and watched as another nurse washed up my son. He squirmed and kicked as she fussed over him. Pretty soon he aimed a thin fountain of pee toward her smiling face. She laughed and ducked, then slapped a diaper on his little bottom. She dressed him in special baby clothes, everything white, then wrapped him in a blue blanket. She carried him over to the window for me to see. My son stared up at me with my own very dark eyes. A thick mop of black curly hair stood up like a brush around his round, fat-cheeked face. He had the stamp of Bauer all over him. No doubt about it. My heart puffed up with pride.

As I peered down at that newborn baby, my eyes got watery. Now, in my day, men did not cry, about anything, not sorrow nor pain, nor the miracle of new life. Even when the doctor had to stitch up my leg after the horseshoe ripped it open, and I felt every needle jab without any painkiller to take the edge off, I never shed a tear. But this was different. This was my son, my firstborn, my namesake. I choked back tears and stared down at the miracle God had given us. Our miracle, Cecile's and my first baby. Even then, I knew he wouldn't be the last baby in our family, bite or no bite!

The nurse holding my son yelled through the window glass. "What's his name, Daddy?"

Daddy! I am a father!

I had to blow my nose before I could answer. "His name is David Bauer, Jr."

Cherish Every Moment.

CHAPTER 7

❧

Real Baby Buggies

Cecile

Whatever happened to real baby buggies? Not the kind that collapse into a diaper bag, or those slick racing model strollers. I mean roomy, plunk down three toddlers, throw in a load of groceries, plus your purse and a change of clothing for each child, baby buggy. What happened to them? The world of Moms and children are the poorer for their disappearance.

When our first child, David Jr., was born, my parents gifted us with a top-of-the-line Thayer. At that time, we lived in an apartment in North Buffalo and it was the best baby buggy in our area. No other family owned such a deluxe model buggy. The price, $35, equaled a working man's weekly salary. Other buggies, made of woven wicker, squeaked as the wheels turned. Our buggy had thick rubber tires (white-walls!), which whispered over the sidewalk cracks and gravel. This carriage of the 1950's was roomy enough for a toddler to sleep prone with arms and legs akimbo. The canvas bonnet sported four metal ribs, which locked into two positions: down to show off the baby; up to guard against sun or rain. The kick board, below the handle of the buggy was called a boot. This boot could be unbuttoned to allow extra kick room for a growing baby.

Since we had no car at that time, this buggy also served as a handy grocery cart. We walked to a local market in the evening and fitted the bags of groceries into the buggy next to our pride and joy, Davy. On the short walk home, we always paused to allow passers-by to coo over our baby.

Fast-forward a few years. Davy is now the oldest of four children. On a bright summer's morning, we decide to go visit my mother. She lives two miles away, too far for my three toddlers to walk, too far for me to carry a squirming infant. Wait a minute! *The buggy.*

"Come on, gang. We are going to Grandma's for lunch."

The kids are hyped up by the prospect of visiting Grandma.

"Grandma? Pancakes!" four-year-old Davy shouts.

"Grandma-pancake!" three-year-old Cathy echoes.

Two-year-old Russ is slow to talk but fast to understand. He knows all about Grandma-pancake. His smile glows. Nine-month-old Barb doesn't care where we are going as long as she gets to ride in the buggy.

We load up. Davy declares himself too old to ride in the buggy. He pitches a fit to prove his maturity. Russ sits in the boot. Barb lolls in the middle. Cathy perches in the prime front position. With the bonnet folded down, she has a clear view of Davy on his tricycle. Our apartment key is tucked into the bottle pocket along with extra diapers. A change of clothing for each child is shoved under the mattress. Our adventure begins.

Military Road in North Buffalo is a busy street, even in the mid 1950's. Cars whiz past as we trundle along the sidewalk. Motorists honk horns in friendly salutes to my happy brood. Davy's tanned legs pump the tricycle pedals. Cathy cheers him on.

"Faster Ravy!" she shouts to her volatile brother. "We are going to Grandma-pancake for lunch!"

Russ waves at the cars. Barb's bottle falls out of her mouth as she dozes. I get a few wolf whistles, *charity whistles,* I think.

We arrive safely at Mother's. We eat a delicious lunch (pancakes what else?), and visit for another hour. Time to walk home. Nap time for everyone, including me.

The two miles home seem endless. Russ and Barb, resolving their sibling rivalry for this brief moment in time, fall asleep curled together at the boot end of the buggy. Cathy rides shotgun, but her shouts of encouragement fail to spur Davy on.

"Faster, Ravy! Nap time!"

He dozes over the handlebars and falls asleep in the middle of Kenmore Avenue. I scoop him up and deposit his limp body beside a scolding Cathy.

"If *I* knew how to ride, I wouldn't fall asleep in the middle of the road!"

Her protest falls on deaf ears. Davy is out for the count.

Now I have a buggy full of small passengers and no one to ride the tricycle home. What to do? Dragging the tricycle as I push the buggy is too exhausting. I am ready for nap time, too. Only one option left. I hook the handlebars of the tricycle over the far end of the buggy and shove onward with my load of a hundred plus pounds of children and ten pounds of cycle. Try doing that with one of those puny fold-into-your-purse strollers!

Cherish Every Moment.

CHAPTER 8

The Rosary Bread

The following autumn, Dave and I decided to take a big step. We moved from our Buffalo apartment to a house in the country. We signed a rent-with-option-to-buy contract for a ranch house in North Collins, thirty miles south of the city. It meant a long commute for Dave, but we wanted our four children to reap the benefits of a country-style upbringing. That first summer in the country, I took advantage of the acre of land behind the house and planted a huge garden. Now we had fresh vegetables for the table and lots of canned tomatoes for winter. Our budget needed all the free food we could manage. We hadn't counted on all the gas dollars Dave would need to spend for his long daily commute. The price of gas in 1958? Thirty cents a gallon!

One week, we were out of our most basic item of food: bread. Payday was four days away and no bread in the house. Even though Jesus said in Matthew's gospel, "Man does not live on bread alone," Matt. 4:4, in our family, if we were out of bread, we were out of food, period!. How could I make Dave's lunch? What would the kids use for their luncheon sandwiches? We had soup, but no crackers to fill in the gaps. What to do? I had plenty of flour, and the other ingredients necessary to bake bread. Unfortunately, previous baking experiences had left me with stone loaves, instead of nice soft edible bread. I stared at my empty bread drawer and prayed.

Mary, mother of God, we need bread. Help me please.

That week a recipe for "fool proof" bread appeared in the daily paper. I had cut out the instructions, just in case a miracle happened and the recipe turned out to *really* be fool proof. That morning I had given Dave my last few quarters so he could buy something for lunch. After his car disappeared down the road, I dug out the ingredients for bread making. *And I prayed.*

The instructions called for eight to ten minutes of kneading. Just long enough for me to pray a decade of the rosary. As I kneaded the bread dough, I slowly prayed ten Hail Mary's.

Need I mention that the bread turned out terrific? Soft and delectable, crispy crusts, with a wonderful texture. My family was raised on this bread. I have used that same recipe for over fifty years now, and it never fails me. *Thanks, Mary.*

Later that same year of the Rosary bread, after the birth of our fifth child, Jean Marie, we moved to a larger house in Eden. We were still settling in that day when a lady from the Welcome Wagon arrived in our driveway. I had mixed up the Rosary bread that morning and the first batch baked in the oven, filling the house with its heavenly aroma. I stared out the back door, as I cleaned the storm door windows.

"Oh no, not another salesman!"

I knew it was edging close to the time when I must drop everything, drag Ravy-Davy into the house, and stand over him while he washed up, then changed into school clothing. Then it would be coax, threaten and shovel his lunch into his reluctant mouth, before shoving him outside in time for the kindergarten school bus. This daily ordeal required split-second timing. A visit from a sales person would certainly foul everything up. My expression must have been less than joyful, because immediately, this woman apologized.

"I know you are busy, settling in and all, but I'm from the Welcome Wagon. I'll only take up a half hour of your time."

"Only?"

She ignored my groan, brushed by me and started up the steps to the kitchen. I remained stubbornly in the back hall, cleaning the windows. I did not worry about her stealing anything. Other than our precious children (and they were playing outside), we had nothing of value to steal! After an embarrassing interval of silence, she came out into the hall and sat on the steps above me.

"Don't let me disturb you," she said cheerfully. I'll talk to you while you work."

She started her sales pitch, explaining all the advantages of Eden, the friendly merchants, eager for our patronage. Every once in a while, she dug out a free gift and offered it to me. I ignored them, so she placed them on the steps in a little pile. When the back door windows gleamed, I went outside to find Davy. He and his younger siblings were racing around the garage in a game of catch me if you can. Cathy was in the lead, pushing the buggy with baby Jean bouncing along. Davy followed right behind them. I nabbed him as he flew past, and dragged him into the house. The saleslady followed me, talking steadily. She talked while Davy washed, talked while I ushered him upstairs to change, talked while I made his lunch.

The timer on the oven rang. *Bread's done.* I pulled on potholder mitts and opened the oven door. The heavenly scent of fresh-baked bread filled the kitchen. As I slid the golden loaves out of the oven, there was a sudden silence behind me. The saleslady drew in a deep breath, then her astonished words washed over me.

"Homemade bread? *Homemade bread!* Don't tell me you make bread? With five children under six, and a new house, yet you have time to make bread? I think that is *marvelous!* Oh, it looks so good."

On and on she raved about the plain white homemade bread, now cooling on the cupboard. You would think I had changed straw to gold to hear her hyperbole. As she went on and on, I softened towards her. Couldn't be rude to a homemade bread fan, now could I? When she left an hour later, she had a still warm loaf of bread, a copy of my recipe, plus my promise to attend the next meeting of the Welcome Wagon Club.

At the meeting, I barely stepped inside the door, when my new friend introduced me to fifty women.

"This is the girl I told you about: the girl with five small children who bakes bread."

I felt like a Betty Crocker clone. Yet, hungry for adult companionship, I belonged to that club for a year before finally giving up in frustration. No one remembered my name. They all called me: "The girl with five small children who bakes bread."

Cherish Every Moment.

The Rosary Bread

This recipe makes ten large loaves of white bread. You will need a large bread pan for mixing up the dough, and enough loaf pans to bake off the loaves. It takes two oven loads to complete the baking. Freezes well.

Ten cups very warm water. One three-pack of yeast. One Tablespoon salt. One cup of sugar. One cup shortening (I use two sticks of margarine, melted). Two bags of white flour.

Dissolve yeast in warm water. Stir in sugar and salt until mixture is cloudy. Dump in 1 bag of flour, stir well. Add the melted shortening. Stir well. Dump in the other bag of flour. Work and squeeze with your hands until you can knead the dough by turning the pan, lifting the dough, and pressing down with the heel of your hands.

Don't worry if your fingers get sticky and coated with dough, that is normal. If the dough seems too stiff (flour remains in the bottom of the pan), add a bit of water. If the dough is too floppy (like pancake batter), add more flour.

Making bread is not rocket science; it is very forgiving. When the consistency of the dough seems workable, knead for ten minutes, about the time it takes to say ten Hail Marys. If you can't pray, watch the clock! It is this step of kneading for ten minutes that makes or breaks the finished product.

After kneading, cover the dough with a clean cloth. Let rise in a warm place until it doubles in size, about sixty minutes. Punch down. Prepare loaf pans by spraying them with cooking spray. When the bread has rested for at least twenty minutes, slick up your hands with margarine, dig into the dough and form large pieces into loaves.

My mother-in-law used to "spank" her loaves to make them nice and smooth. When all the dough is formed into loaves, cover all with a clean cloth and let rise another hour.

Bake at 350 degrees for about 35 minutes. Cool before freezing. Enjoy!

CHAPTER 9

❧❧❧

The Lean Years

Back in the dark ages, when Dave and I were young newly-weds, God made his presence known in no uncertain terms. Baby every year? Of course. We felt it was God's will that we have a large family. We accepted the children with love and gratitude but struggled to pay the bills. In our seventh year of marriage, our family numbered five children under age six. We moved from our single story ranch home in North Collins to a larger, two-story house in Eden. The house contained three bedrooms, with room to expand. Good thing, the way our family kept growing! Our tight budget took a direct hit, but we were managing. Then the tax bill came.

I opened the envelope with a sinking heart. "Ninety dollars and ten cents!"

Our budget was so tight it squeaked! October brought the yearly house insurance bill, plus school expenses for a child in Catholic school. Add to that the cost of clothing and food for a family of seven? How would we ever pay this vital expense? If we ignored the bill, the county could foreclose on our house for unpaid taxes. The dime I could manage to find, but ninety dollars?

In those days of the late 1950's, ninety dollars might just as well been a thousand dollars for all the spare money we didn't have, or even hope to have. I prayed, oh how I prayed for a miracle. For Dave to get a raise. For someone to drop a hundred dollar bill in our mailbox. Something, anything, so we wouldn't lose our house.

The day the taxes were due, I scrubbed the kitchen floor with my tears. I was pregnant again, and so desperate I would have sold my clothing to raise the money. *Better to be naked than to be homeless,* I thought, as I dumped out the dirty water. The mailman tooted outside.

"Just more bills," I muttered, sniffling as I waddled out to the mailbox.

A long envelope waited in the rural box. I opened it in the driveway as I started back to the house. Into my shaking hands fell a check from a magazine for ninety dollars, *the exact amount we needed for our tax bill.*

I gasped and stood still, weaving with joy and astonishment. Two prayers answered at the same moment. Not only did the check represent payment for my very first published story; but it meant we could pay our tax bill! I stared around at the suddenly beautiful day. My friend and neighbor, Betty Schichtel, mother of seven children, the *best* mother I ever met, waved from her front lawn.

"Good news?" she called, with a smile.

"The best!" I said, too overcome with gratitude to speak normally. "Tell you later, OK?"

In the woods surrounding our country home, the maples shimmered with gold and crimson beauty. Wild grapes, glistening with royal color, tangled and wrapped around the branches of pine trees (free fruit for making jelly!). The late autumn sun warmed my aching shoulders, shoulders which suddenly grew straighter as I realized the magnitude of God's gifts. A few feet away, our house (the home we would occupy for over twenty-five years and raise our ten children in) never looked more beautiful to me. Inside the toddlers were waking up from their naps.

"Mommy!" Jean, the youngest, called out, her voice a sweet reminder of God's multitude of blessings. I glanced again at the check in my shaking hands, a gift from above, the answer to a desperate mother's prayer. God is good!

Cherish Every Moment.

CHAPTER 10

❧

Go Fly a Kite

Our family was blessed in many ways, but one gift I really appreciated was the fact I could be a stay-at-home Mom for the first ten years of childbearing. I set my own work schedule: laundry three times a week, bake bread every other day, make jam at my leisure, clean the house on the weekends (while supervising the older children as they cleaned their bedrooms). It was a wonderful time of life for me. We were severely budget challenged, of course, but I was rich in *time.* Time to try new recipes, time to visit with Betty, our next door neighbor who also had a large family, time to write short stories and articles for the local paper. Time to teach the children how to jump rope and the numerous rhymes that accompanied the swinging rope. Time for vigorous games of kick ball and badminton. Time for woods' walking and berry picking across the road from our country home. Time to fly a kite!

Something about springtime brought out the kite flying weirdness in me. Yes, I knew I needed to be spring cleaning, washing walls, cutting my fingers cleaning the Venetian blinds, scrubbing the rug in the living room, waxing the wall to wall hardwood floors, sorting through the winter coats and bringing out the summer shorts for the family. Eventually I would accomplish all that drudgery, but first, as soon as the stiff warm breezes of springtime stirred the budding lilacs, it was time to fly a kite.

Usually I waited until the older children were in school (didn't want to embarrass them!) and the younger were ones down for their naps before I assembled my kite and headed for the open fields behind our house.

What a beautiful day! Green grasses beneath my feet, trees adorned with pink buds gleaming in the woods beyond, and blue sky above. The kite kicked in my hands as it rose in red and green splendor toward the heavens. My blah spirits lifted in tandem with the soaring paper stretched over the thin sticks formed into a cross. No tail, my kites always flew better without them. How it dove and rose again as I worked the string.

As the kite soared, the string tugged on my fingers, just as God's springtime renewal tugged on my winter weariness. Forgotten were the memories of my aching back from shoveling the driveway, the draining illnesses that laid low all of the children (Measles, Chicken Pox, even Scarlet Fever), my own bouts of bronchitis and pneumonia, the sleepless nights hovering over sick children. All those bad memories blew away, leaving my mind clear and filled with joy.

Kite flying took me back to my youth, made me smile and thank God for my blessings. Distractions, thankfully, were few. Our good neighbor, Betty Schichtel, waved as she loaded up their station wagon with her passel of children.

"Don't forget, Well Baby Clinic next Monday," she called across the back field.

I grinned, anticipating Monday's excursion in Schichtel's station wagon. Six or seven toddlers loaded into the back seat, all chattering together in that delightful childish language that only toddlers understand. Betty driving. Me, a lifelong non-smoker, watching in awe as she somehow managed to light a cigarette in the brief pause between shifting from second to third gear on her car. Betty remained, always, an awesome woman. We lost her to cancer in 1964.

But that sad day would be years away. This spring day, I smiled and waved in silence. Sure didn't want to wake up my sleeping toddlers right now. Spoil a perfect kite-flying afternoon? No way! Betty's car waited at the end of their driveway for the bus to pass. The kindergarten bus driver tipped his cap as he dropped off our number three child. Russ ran toward me to watch the colorful kite soar. The oil delivery man tooted his horn as he roared past our property. The mail carrier grinned as he slid yet another rejection letter into our mailbox.

Who cares? Time to fly a kite!

Cherish Every Moment.

CHAPTER 11

Wish You Were Here

Our second daughter, Barbara, the fourth child of our marriage, came into this life with nary a cry to mark her passage. The doctor and nurses were amazed that this newborn stared around with the eyes of a wise old lady, and merely gurgled a grudging approval of everyone around her. Barb was an amazingly good baby. She slept through the night at six weeks, emptied her bottles with gusto, and seemed to have a surprisingly mature, if haughty, view of our mostly noisy family. Oldest son Dave had such a wild temper, we nicknamed him Ravy-Davy. Second born, Cathy, was so determined to be independent, that when thwarted by her limited skill at dressing herself or tying her shoes, she often had what parents today call, *Melt-downs*. Being a very young mother then, I assumed that all little girls were like Cathy: strong, independent, needing very little help from the mothering department. Russ, the third born, seemed contented to sit with thumb in mouth, watching the wild entertainment provided by his noisy siblings.

And Barbara? She watched everything with the wise eyes of a pragmatic old soul. Nobody ever knew what Barb was thinking. She kept her opinions to herself, seldom cried, yet her little shoulders were squared back. That proud posture revealed a hidden determination to do things *her way.* If I had been more mature, I might have realized that each child born into our rapidly growing family needed my individual attention, regardless of how they might try to fake their own strengths. But I was so young and inexperienced, only 23, and the mother of six children. *What did I know?*

From the age of three, Barb always fixed her own breakfast, cereal, or bread and jelly. I left the bowls down on the cupboard so the children could help themselves, in case I had a diaper to change, or a bottle to warm up for the newest member of our family. Every year or two, we welcomed another blessing from heaven.

One morning I forgot the bowls. Barbara was usually one of the first children up, and she always awoke hungry. But this morning, her older siblings had eaten first, toast and eggs, made by Ravy-Davy, who prided himself on not breaking the yolks as he assembled eggs for sunny-side up. He and Cathy were making their lunches for school, peanut butter and jelly sandwiches on homemade bread. Russ hung around my chair as I bottle-fed Rose. He ran a tiny play car up and down the arms of the big padded chair I used as a baby-feeding station. Echoing down the stairwell were the cries of fifth-born child, Jean, as she howled from her crib upstairs.

So much to do, so little of me to do it! I thought. As our only breadwinner, Dave worked long hours. Most mornings, he left for his job as a tow-truck driver before the children were up. Many nights he returned after they were safely tucked into bed. Chaos in the house? My job. I heaved a long, tired sigh and jiggled the bottle to wake up the dozing baby, Rose.

Barbara scampered down the steps and hurried into the kitchen. Minutes later, I heard a soft exclamation from the kitchen.

"Everything OK out there?" I called out.

No answer. Davy and Cathy hurried out the kitchen door. Beside me, Russ ran to the window to watch the school bus tooting its horn at the end of the driveway. The back door slammed. Silence from the kitchen. I got up from the chair, still holding Rose, busy polishing off her bottle, and walked into the kitchen. Barb sat at the table with a box of cereal. She brought up fists full of dry cereal and stuffed them into her mouth. A single tear dripped down her plump cheek.

"Oh, honey, I'm sorry. I forgot to put the cereal bowls down this morning. Want some milk with that?"

She nodded. Another tear escaped down her cheek. Juggling the baby over my shoulder, I brought down a bowl, and fetched the milk bottle (we actually had milk bottles then, back in the good old days!) out of the refrigerator. The sugar bowl was already on the table. Barb hurried to the drawer and plucked out a spoon. She insisted on pouring the cereal.

In our large family, independence was a valued trait encouraged in all the children. As soon as a child seemed old enough, he or she was taught to do many mundane things. Davy learned to fry eggs at age six. Cathy managed to make toast without burning herself, morning after morning. Russ could butter his own bread, as long as someone else sliced it from the loaf. The older ones helped the younger ones, always. After Barb spooned sugar over her oat cereal, I poured milk from the almost full half-gallon glass container. Some of it splashed onto the plastic tablecloth. Barb stared at it, a frightened expression on her little angel face. For once I could almost read her mind, *we don't waste milk in this house!* A silent echo of my own voice prickled my conscience.

I opened my mouth to give reassurances, "Don't worry, Barb, even Mom makes a mess sometimes." But at that moment, a thump and a cry of pain announced that toddler Jean had managed to climb out of her crib and land on her soggy bottom. I hurried to the stairway, intent on rescuing Jean. Barb's worried expression was brushed aside in the rush and fuss of a mother too busy to take time to investigate her daughter's unusual behavior.

As I leaped up the stairs, newborn baby held tightly on my shoulder, bawling toddler screaming from her bedroom, I did muse briefly on Barb's surprising tears at the breakfast table.

Barb never cries! I thought. But then the frantic morning rolled on without another pause to allow me to really contemplate my mature three-year-old and her out-of-character tears.

When we returned to the kitchen, baby Rose sound asleep in my arms, Jean dry, dressed, and ravenous, Barb's little face had cleared of the worry lines. She glanced up as the three of us entered the kitchen, sighed deeply, and ducked her head as she dug into the cereal.

It was bath time that evening before I discovered the hideous burn mark on Barb's arm. The shape of a Christmas tree cookie, the crimson scar seemed to shimmer cruelly in the brightly lit bathroom.

"What happened, Barbie-doll? How did you burn yourself like this?"

She ducked her head and a single tear slid down her rosy cheeks. I remembered then the puzzling scene at the breakfast table, the soft exclamation in the kitchen while I fed the baby.

"Did the toaster do this?" I said, careful to blame a kitchen appliance, not her. No need for me to accuse her. She did that herself, with copious tears.

"I climbed on the cupboard to get a bowl. Davy and Cathy were too busy to help. I'm sorry, Mom. I won't do it again."

Immediately, the cruel sting of a bad mother's guilt raked my soul. My little girl's burn vividly accused me of being too busy, too strict, so rule-bound that my little girl was afraid to tell me she burned herself. She hid the pain rather than risk my angry words over a minor rule infraction: climbing on the cupboard.

I gave Barb a quick hug. "Honey, next time tell me if you get hurt. You didn't have to suffer all day. We do have burn ointment, you know!"

She nodded and bit her lips as I dressed her flaming wound. But the die was cast. This daughter never did feel confident enough of my approval to tell me of her pain or ask for my help. For anything.

Fast forward twenty-plus years. Daughter Jean had moved to California. The sisters had always been close. Soon Barb moved out West, also. Now in her early twenties, Barb had not changed into a tell-all-to-Mom daughter, not at all. Dave and I never realized that the first man she married, a hidden alcoholic who cursed her on the wedding night, had also beaten her frequently thereafter. We did hear about the divorce, actually an annulment, after Barb endured a long, painful, year of martial hell on earth. True to form, she never complained about it to us. Later, she married a good man, and soon Barb became pregnant. Her baby was due in November, six months after Rose gave birth to Larry.

We kept in touch via hand written letters. No email in those days, just snail-mail. I wrote about Larry's birth, how Rose had managed to give birth without drugs, and how thrilling it was for me to be able to cut the umbilical cord.

By the time November drew near, our letters became more frequent. I could tell by the tone of Barb's letters, the unsaid words as well as the carefully crafted, try-hard-to-be-cheerful phrases, that she was scared. A long way from California to Western New York.

Then came the letter that brought tears to my eyes. Toward the end of a brightly written letter detailing all the happy events, the planning, the shopping, the baby shower given by her in-laws, Barb wrote: *Wish you were here, Mom.*

Oh, how I wished I could have flown out there to hold her hand during the birth of her first baby! But Rose and Larry still lived with us. I held down two jobs at that time, waitress at night and school bus driver during the day. I also took care of the infant, Larry, weekday mornings, so Rose could work days. It was a grueling schedule. *Would we never get those bills paid?* I really had no choice. I would have given an arm or a leg to be able to take off and go to Barb to witness the birth of her little girl, but it didn't happen. I regret it to this day. Being with Barb when she asked for my help for the first time would have been a memory to cherish forever.

Thank God, the good Lord gives us second chances! Several years later, after Dave and I also moved to the West Coast, I was privileged to be at the birth of Barb's son. Yes, she asked me to be there. Yes, I held her hand, and yes it was wonderful!

Cherish Every Moment.

CHAPTER 12

Shoe Store Blues

Back in the early 1960's, before Target and Walmart made one-stop shopping a household term, when people needed shoes, you went to a *Shoe Store*. This was a magical place of tall walls with white boxes of shoes stacked to the ceiling. Comfy chairs lined up from the front entrance to the back of the store. Best of all, shoe stores had real salespeople. These hard working clerks measured each foot, and then fetched out various pairs of shoes, no matter how long it took, until the customer chose a suitable pair of new footwear.

A beautiful shopping experience, unless you had a passel of children in tow.

By mismanagement or grim coincidence, six of our seven children needed new shoes simultaneously. A budget breaker, but incontestable, the children needed shoes! Leaving baby Jason with Grandma, I took the kids shopping for footwear. A sign in the window of Buster Brown Shoes looked promising. *Bring the baby in for his shoes. We don't mind the noise.* All right, they asked for it. I drew a deep breath, hoisted toddler Rose on my hip, and walked in trailing children.

60

The clerk greeted us warmly. The welcome sight of six children needing shoes must have started sweet music in his ears. The anticipated sound of the cash register ringing made him smile. The children lined up, as they often did, according to age. Davy was first. As the clerk measured his foot, number one son began his campaign.

"I want black shoes with no laces, because I'm always breaking my shoe laces and Mom never remembers to buy black ones, and I have to use brown ones, and the kids at school make fun of me because I have black shoes with brown laces, and ..."

By that time, the clerk had returned with a popular new item. Snap-Jacks (shoes without laces, the tongue snapped down to fasten the shoe onto the child's foot). Trying them on a delighted Davy, he remarked casually, "Very smart, Mother. No laces to break or replace. Only $8.95."

I answered, not so casually. "Nine dollars for a pair of shoes that will be outgrown in eight to ten weeks?" Remember this was in the good old days of 1961, when the cost of children's shoes averaged around three dollars a pair. I shook my head. "Bring him a pair of black oxfords and some extra laces."

I silenced Davy's protests with a dark look that meant *take it or wear brown laces in your old shoes!* He accepted the black oxfords, grumbling darkly under his breath.

Next customer, Cathy. She asked for patent leather pumps with skinny heels. She received gray oxfords with pink laces. After much discussion and sulking, Russ settled for brown oxfords with plaid laces.

Sweet Barbie was the easiest to please. Anything, as long as it was new and shiny lit up her day. She loved her red buckle sandals.

The clerk came to Jean. Suspiciously Jean eyed the clerk and his foot-measuring tool. Loudly, she protested the removal of her old shoe. Stubbornly, she defied all efforts to try on new shoes. Jean didn't *want* new shoes. She didn't *need* new shoes. She liked her *old* shoes just fine.

The clerk looked to me for help. "Do you think a lollipop might help change her mind?"

I shrugged. "Maybe a box of cough drops? It takes her quite a while to open them."

Naturally, the shoe store didn't carry cough drops, but he sent an assistant down the block to a nearby drug store. Meanwhile, he turned to Rose who had been intently studying the proceedings. Having grasped the main idea, namely that shoes were being removed and replaced, she was well prepared. Her shoes were off, ditto her socks, and all the children searching the entire store failed to find them again. The clerk eyed me suspiciously.

"She had socks and shoes on when we came in, honest!" I said defensively.

He laughed rather weakly. "Guess my assistant must have placed them in an empty box and put them away by mistake."

We all gazed at the shelves lined with hundreds of white shoe boxes. From floor to ceiling, like stoic soldiers lined up for inspection, the anonymous boxes kept their secrets. The clerk sighed and shook his head.

"I'll give her a new pair of socks, free of charge. OK?"

Rose was wearing little pink socks and new white toddler shoes, when the assistant returned with a box of cough drops for stubborn Jean. A brief heated exchange between the clerk and his assistant failed to turn up Rose's old socks and shoes. Jean, contentedly bribed, allowed the man to measure her foot and try on red sandals like Barb's. *Mission accomplished!*

After paying the weary clerk for all six pairs of shoes (took the better part of a twenty dollar bill!), we left the store. I hoisted Rose on my hip, with a firm grip on her new shoes. Children trailed behind me like little sheep, each carrying his or her precious box of new shoes. We all turned to wave to the nice, friendly clerk who had been so helpful. As we raised our hands to thank him, I noticed the assistant removing the *Bring the baby...we don't mind the noise,* sign out of the window. As we watched, he ripped it up and tossed it into the wastebasket.

Cherish Every Moment.

Front (left to right): Barbara, Jean, Rose
Back *(left to right)*: Davy, Cathy, Rusty

CHAPTER 13

꧁✦꧂

Cooking Lessons, One through Ten

As mentioned in a previous chapter, each of our children learned his or her way around the kitchen at an early age. Davy, the first-born, learned to make fried eggs at age six. Because we had an electric stove, my teaching about using this appliance safely was tailored to provide maximum safety. There would be no more burns, like the shameful scar on little Barb's arm. Davy seemed eager to learn how to make his hot breakfast.

"I'm tired of cold cereal," he said, an echo of his father's words. Dad enjoyed eggs every morning. Davy wanted the same.

"OK, Davy, get out the fry pan."

We used a small iron skillet for eggs. He dug it out of the bottom drawer of the stove and handed it to me. I put it on the smallest burner, the left back one, because the knob was directly above the burner and easy for a six-year-old to reach. I showed him the markings on the black knob.

"H means high. Turn it on high." He did so. "Now, Davy, it will take a few minutes for the burner to heat up. Put a bit of butter into the pan to melt and wait until it sizzles (This was BCS before cooking spray). While you are waiting, break your eggs into this cup."

I demonstrated how to crack the shells onto the rim of the cup. He poked his fingers into the shells, breaking both the yolks. Eggs and a bit of shell dropped into the coffee mug. His face darkened. He was mad at himself for not doing it right.

"That's all right, Davy. When the yolks break, you just make scrambled eggs instead of Dippy eggs."

My kids called sunny side up eggs by their own private label, *Dippy eggs,* which meant eggs with unbroken yokes capable of being dipped into by homemade toast.

I handed him a wooden spoon and let him pour the eggs into the pan.

"Now, with an electric stove, as soon as the eggs hit the pan, you can turn off the burner because there is enough heat now to finish cooking the eggs."

He nodded, stirring vigorously. He wore oversized pot holder mitts on each hand. A serious expression wrinkled his narrow forehead and clouded his sparkling brown eyes. *My little chef!*

"That's it, the eggs are done. Pull the pan off the burner. Careful, don't burn yourself."

His smile of triumph as he dug a fork into, "My own eggs!" made all the careful instructions well worth it. Later, of course, he grew more skillful at breaking the eggs and had the pleasure of making his very own Dippy eggs. Naturally, he lorded it over his younger siblings.

"Mom taught me how to cook!"

Each of the children, as they expressed an interest in cooking, learned the secret of making eggs, or whatever they craved at that moment in time. Cathy never cared for eggs. She wanted to learn to make the important stuff: desserts. We started with gelatin and she was very good about stirring and adding bananas to the mix. Later she graduated to making pudding. One day she decided to make a Wicky-Wacky Cake. This recipe came from her Cooking Class in school and seemed to be a favorite of every one of her classmates.

"It's easy, Cathy," they reassured her.

She seemed confident as she assembled the ingredients in our kitchen. Careful not to burn herself, she melted a stick of butter, then added cocoa powder, flour, eggs and other ingredients to the mix. She poured it into an oblong cake pan, then slid it into the oven. We all waited for the cake to bake. The younger children sat around the kitchen table, forks at the ready, eager to taste the cake with the weird name. We waited. I helped Cathy wash up the baking dishes. We waited.

Something is wrong. We should be smelling chocolate cake by now, I thought.

"Did you turn on the oven, Cathy?" Russ asked, impatiently licking his empty fork

"Yes, I turned on the oven," she snapped, her face red with anger.

"So where is the Wicky Wacky Cake?" he persisted.

Davy chimed in. "The Wicky Wacky Cake made by wicky wacky Cathy!"

Cathy threw the drying towel at him. He dodged away and ran out the back door, chortling.

"Wicky wacky Cathy!"

The younger children took up the chant. When Cathy started after them, they too, ran out the back door, giggling. I stayed behind to check the cake in the oven. Carefully I opened the oven door. *Stone cold.* The cake looked just the same now as it had when Cathy slid it onto the oven rack. I checked the oven control. Yep, it showed 350 degrees. But no heat rose from the darkness of the oven. I turned to Cathy.

"Sorry, Cathy. Guess the oven gave up."

She burst into tears. "You mean I blew it up! I can't do anything right," she raged, and stalked out of the room. Her stomping steps up the stairway to her bedroom echoed through the house.

Today, if any of her siblings want to provoke a reaction from Cathy, they have only to mutter, *"Wicky Wacky Cathy."* Then, they stand back as she flies into a predictable, embarrassed rage. But at least she is old enough now to laugh about it too.

Russ never took much interest in cooking lessons. His favorite food consisted of homemade bread and jam. Yet, just because he never asked for cooking advice, doesn't mean he wasn't watching, and learning in his own quiet way.

One snowy winter's Saturday, bread-baking day in our house, I needed to run an errand. Because we lived out in the country, any store-related errand meant my absence from the kitchen for at least ninety minutes. On a bad driving winter day, it took longer. I left Barbara in charge of baking off the bread. The ten loaves were waiting on the cupboard, predictably rising in the warmth of the house.

The girls were rearranging their bedroom upstairs. The boys were roller skating down cellar. I set the kitchen timer to remind Barb to put the first load of bread into the oven. It took two loads to bake off all ten loaves.

According to the stories I heard later, Barb baked the first five loaves with no problem. She slid them into the oven, set the timer, and went back upstairs. When the timer went off, she returned to unload and reload the oven with the last five loaves. This time she forgot to set the timer. Busy arguing with Cathy and Jean about this week's arrangement of their bedroom (they changed the placement of the furniture every week, it seemed), no one noticed when something began to smell burned in the kitchen. *Burned bread!*

Russ was the first to notice. He opened the oven door to let the dark smoke roll out and yelled up the stairs to his sisters. "Who's in charge of the bread? It's burning down here!"

Three sisters galloped down the steps. They all gasped, horrified, at the sight of five scorched loaves of bread smoking in the kitchen sink. No one was more upset than Barb, who burst into tears.

"Mom's going to kill me!" she sobbed.

Her sisters tried to comfort her. Russ didn't help much as he continued to moan.

"Five loaves of bread, wasted! All that good bread that Mom worked so hard to mix up, all burned up and gone!"

"What are you belly-aching about, Russ?" Cathy demanded. "You didn't make the bread, Mom did."

Jean piped up. "Maybe we can make more bread? I watched her make it lots of times. It doesn't look so hard to do, just messy."

"Yeah," Cathy said. "You have to get your hands into the dough and squish around and fight with it." *Cathy didn't do messy.*

Timid Barb backed away. "I could never do it like Mom does. Too hard. I would ruin it."

Meanwhile, Russ had been staring at the big bag of flour in the corner of the hallway.

"I'll do it," he said. As the family member who would miss the bread the most, he decided to step up and be a hero to his siblings. Plus, he reasoned, if we ran out of homemade bread during the week, it was store bread until Saturday's baking again. *A horrible thought!*

When I returned from shopping after waiting in a long line to replace a faulty high chair for our baby, Jim, I found the kitchen spotless. Yet, the older children seemed strangely quiet.

"Thanks, guys, for cleaning up the kitchen," I said, a bit mystified.

I glanced around the cupboard area. Five perfectly formed loaves of baked bread waited on the counter. But there were also several pretty pitiful loaves of bread rising in the pans. It looked as if the yeast had failed in those other loaves because the dough barely hit the halfway mark on the pans.

"What happened to the bread?" I asked, puzzled.

The older children glanced at each other. No one said a word at first. Barb burst into tears and ran up the stairs to her bedroom. Cathy started to giggle. Russ blushed. He wouldn't meet my eyes. Jean bit her lips to keep from tattling. Finally Davy stuck his head into the kitchen. As the oldest, he wasn't afraid to be a nark.

"The first bread burned. Russ tried to make more, but I think he did it wrong."

I examined the very short loaves. Pretty lame, as the kids would say. But the dough looked smooth, and well kneaded.

"Did you put yeast in it, Russ?" I asked. He nodded, as puzzled as the rest of the kitchen crew. "What else did you put into the mix?"

"I made it just like you do," he said, counting off ingredients on his fingers. "Water, salt, yeast, flour, melted butter, and more flour. Then fight with it for ten minutes."

My turn to giggle at his description of the kneading of bread dough. I patted his arm, which still held bits of sticky bread dough around the wrist area.

"Good try, Russ. But you need to put sugar in the mix, because the yeast feeds on it. Without sugar, the bread dough won't rise."

He looked crestfallen. "Oh."

I went upstairs to comfort Barb. "Every cook makes mistakes, even Grandma Ramier," I reminded her.

My mother came to visit one beautiful fall day and decided to make apple pie. I kept my salt and sugar in unmarked yellow canisters on the kitchen counter. You guessed it, she grabbed the salt and used it as sugar for the pies. Oh, how she stomped around and berated herself for, "Wasting all those good apples."

We had other kitchen disasters as the years fled past and the children learned to cook. Jean's first attempt at making biscuits ended up in a tirade as her younger brothers used the resulting tough in-edibles as hockey pucks. Rose, busy making cookies one day, bent down too close to the batter and ended up snagging her long blonde hair in the beaters. But they did all learn to cook, especially when they mastered making a favored food.

Whenever I pulled the station wagon up to the back door and yelled up the steps, "Groceries (I pronounced it growk-gries). Come and get them," children rushed to unload the shopping bags.

"Oh good," Jean always said, "Ingredients!"

Jean's pancakes were legendary. Mike specialized in scrambled egg sandwiches. Four eggs scrambled, stacked between large slices of fresh homemade bread. One bite and the eggs fell out the other side! We bought eggs by the three dozen flat in those days. Jay loved bread pudding. Tom wanted macaroni and cheese. In fact, the year he married Lynette, a very lean year for Tom and his wife, they lived on mac & cheese for twelve months! Jim loved French toast and learned to make it before age ten. He even taught his cousins how to make it. Grandson Larry learned how to make grilled cheese sandwiches while vacationing here as a boy. Velveeta sliced thick, between slabs of homemade bread, with thinly sliced onion between the layers, then grilled on my pancake griddle.

I joked with Larry's father one day. "I hope you don't mind. We converted Larry." When he looked so alarmed (Larry's dad is not a church-going person), I added, "We converted Larry to onionizm."

As the children grew up and left home, I presented each of them with a copy of my homemade cookbook, *Family Favorites.* I believe they still follow the many recipes that I used when they were children. In fact, the other day, Russ called. "How do you make chicken and rice, Mom?"

"Check your cookbook, Son."

Cherish Every Moment.

CHAPTER 14

の※の

The Feeding and Nourishing of a Large Family

Every time someone learns we are the parents of ten children, they invariably ask, "How did you manage with such a large family? Just buying food for all those people boggles the mind."

I have no idea how we managed to meet expenses in those good old days. Dave worked for minimum wage. I stayed home to take care of the kids. We cut corners wherever we could. God looked out for us. Somehow, the bills were paid on time. The children always had nice clothes to wear, even if many of them were hand-me-downs (the large leaf bags they usually arrived in were labeled by our girls: *Goodie bags*). We ate three square meals every day, and sometimes even had ice cream for special occasions like birthdays. We managed.

On one occasion our local paper, *The Buffalo Evening News*, featured a food column that offered to help housewives "stretch your food budget." The column's author asked women to send in a form with the number of people in the family, and their weekly food budget. The columnist would then prepare a detailed, cost-

72

cutting food budget for the reader. I mailed in my form listing the size of our family and the amount of money we had to buy food. Several weeks later, a reply came in the mail.

> *Dear Mrs. Bauer. It is impossible to feed all those people with the amount of money in your food budget. Sorry I couldn't help you.*

I chuckled all day. Because, with or without the help of the columnist, we were doing the impossible. The children were well fed and we weren't in debt to anyone except the bank holding the mortgage on our house.

It helped tremendously that the USDA, a government run commodities give-away for low income families, supplied us with certain Surplus Food. Every month, we loaded up the pre-school children, lots of boxes and bags, and drove to a nearby Fire Hall to pick up our bonanza of free food. We were given real butter, flour, cornmeal, peanut butter, cheese, powdered eggs, canned pork (really yummy), powdered milk, and whatever else the government bought from farmers for the program. Each family member received one of something. For example, with a family of twelve, we received twelve pounds of butter, twelve pounds of cheese, many cans of peanut butter, and canned meat, two or three bags of flour, etc. We might be down to our last dollar but we always had food in the house!

So when the cupboard looked bare of essentials like cookies or other treats, I had the ingredients to bake up whatever suited the children's desires. One year, they clamored for Christmas cookies. I had never baked these special treats after that one failure when I was still a newlywed. Homemade bread and chocolate birthday cake were my specialities, but I was willing to try.

The school children were home for a Snow Day when the

first tray of white cut-out cookies slid out of the oven. The recipe made at least a hundred, so the kitchen table sported edge-to-edge cookies. Our wonderful neighbor, Betty Schicktel, gave me the recipe for a butter frosting. It used butter, powdered milk, and powdered sugar. My only cost was the powdered sugar, which in those days had a price tag of thirty-nine cents. As soon as the last cookie cooled enough for young hands to touch, the marathon frosting session began. Oldest son, Davy, demanded the job of Frosting King. He slathered on the frosting, the other children put on the sprinkles. What a licking good time they all had! I peeked over my shoulder occasionally, as I mixed up gingerbread cookies for the next batch of cut-out cookies.

What a great time they are having! We should have started this tradition years ago.

By the time the cookies were baked, frosted, sprinkled, and stored away in our biggest picnic cooler, all the children wore frosting and multi-colored sprinkle stains on their happy faces. Davy finished up the last of the frosting by making a frosting sandwich!

When Daddy Dave came home that evening, he stopped in the kitchen doorway and sniffed the pungent air.

"Ah," he said, "Cookies! Now it smells like Christmas around here."

On Christmas day, we usually hosted the family party. It was easier that way for me. No need to bundle up all those kids, and then have to keep an eagle eye on the pack of them at Grandma's house. Amazing how much trouble they could get into while attending a party away from home! One year, at my mother's house, the children were seated in the den, while the adults crowded around the kitchen table. Because my mother's kitchen was so small with scant counter space, she had to keep her pies in the den. When the adults finished the delicious turkey dinner with all the trimmings, Grandma Ramier went into the den to fetch out the pies. She returned to the kitchen laughing, with the pie pans in her hands.

"Look," she said, grinning, "The kids helped themselves already!"

One apple pie was almost gone, the pumpkin pie had two pieces removed. I blushed as everyone laughed.

Dave chuckled. "You know, Grandma, those children are trained to be independent, and they do know how to help themselves!"

From that year on, we hosted the Christmas party at our house! Sister Betty and husband Len brought our mother out to our country home. My brother Jim, married and with two young children, also came for Christmas dinner. Oldest sister Joy and Ed never came for dinner, but they sometimes arrived later for the fun and games. Another latecomer was my cousin Leo, younger brother of Huck (who introduced Dave and me at the dance that long ago occasion). Leo and his family lived in the Western New York area. During Christmas holidays, they went down to Pennsylvania to visit relatives, then stopped at our house on the way back.

We loved having a houseful of people for Christmas. Grandma R., Betty and Len always brought gifts for the kids. Which meant that after supper, we had a second Christmas gift exchange. The kids were so excited that they could barely contain themselves as Betty and I did up the dishes from the feast. It was the house rule that on Christmas, the children are given a holiday from their scheduled chores. Mom always does the dishes. That meant that while Betty and I chatted over a sink full of my better dishes (as opposed to the everyday ones which often got broken before their time!), children leaned into the kitchen, panting with greed.

"Aren't you done, yet?"

Funny thing, they never offered to help to speed up the pro-cess. Finally, the kitchen looked good, the dishes washed, dried and put away. Time to open gifts. Wrapping paper flew, children exclaimed in delight, adults grinned. It was Christmas, after all. When the last torn paper hit the trash, the kids put their new treasures under the tree already crowded with gifts. Then they raced for the basement and their snow suits and boots. Time to go sled-riding! By the time the last child slammed the back door, the adults were already playing cards. Sometimes we played Charades or Twister. One year we rolled up the rug and had an impromptu square dance. What a great play time we adults had as our chil-dren rode down the snowy hills out back.

Sooner or later, the children returned, rosy of cheeks, fam-ished again. Time for the cookie parade. One year, as the children (and grandchildren by that time) paraded down the long hall to the master bedroom where the cookie chest lived, Leo happened to be watching. *Hmmm, children walk down that hallway, and they come back with fists full of cookies!*

Soon a taller version of a child also joined the cookie parade. Leo retained that child-like manner for as long as I can remember. When my brother died suddenly, and I was weeping because I had no brother now, Leo leaned close to whisper. *"I'll be your brother now, Cecile,"* he said, and gave me a big hug. *Thanks Leo, I needed that.*

Cherish Every Moment.

❧❧❧

CHAPTER 15

The Incredible Chili Sit-in and Other Table Talk

With our large family of stair-step children, our kitchen table stayed pretty full at mealtime. My father built us a seven-foot-long table and a long bench for one side. Our four kitchen chairs, plus two stools and a highchair completed the table seating arrangements. The bench held a passel of children, lined up cheek by jowl, forks or spoons at the ready, appetites keen, for whatever food hit their plates. I did a lot of one-dish type meals: spaghetti, chili, macaroni and cheese, etc. Very few of the children turned down the meal of the day. Barb did hate chili as a baby, but she learned to love it as a toddler.

Mealtime began with the saying of "Grace Before Meals." Everyone stood with hands folded until the *Amen*, and then scrambled to their usual places, ready to eat. At that time, our oldest son, Davy, sat in the far corner, across the long table from Dad, and next to Tom who occupied one of the stools. One night, I dished up the chili from the big pot, including Davy's bowl, even though he was late coming in from sled-riding. He just had to take one last ride down the big hill before dark chased the children home for supper. I heard the back door slam and his hurried feet on the basement steps as he shed wet winter clothing and mittens.

"Sorry, Mom. Be right up," he called, and soon appeared in the doorway.

His face gleamed ruddy from the cold night air and a bit of snow still dripped from his dark hair. He scrambled across Tom, who had to lean back, spoon in hand, to let his older brother squeeze past him. Somehow, between the tight quarters of the chairs pressed too close to the table, and his careless scramble to his seat, Davy sat down into his bowl of chili!

What a howling of laughter from the peanut gallery on the bench! Davy's already flushed face got even redder. I scooped up the mashed food into the dog's dish, and he hurried upstairs to change his pants. Good thing I always made lots of chili, ya think? Even now, decades later, the family still talks about the great chili sit-in.

Later that year, we were all assembled at the table for an ordinary evening meal. Tom, in his place at the end of the table, began to howl. *What now?*

"Everybody's looking at me!" he sobbed.

Of course, now everyone *was* looking at him.

When questioned later, Tom said, "Every time I looked up, someone was staring at me. I thought I had done something bad, or had food on my face, or something. It made me sad."

So gave rise to one of our family's favorite expressions. If someone is acting outrageous, maybe seeking attention by being pesky, we say, *"What's the matter? Nobody looking at you?"*

Back in the children's school days, occasionally, someone would bring home a friend from school for what parents today call a *play date*. It mattered little to my meal planning. I routinely cooked for an army every day. Always room for a couple more people, big or small. One evening we had a little visitor, a girl friend of Barb's, I think. At that time our girls wore their hair in what they called a pageboy cut. Straight bangs across their foreheads, hair cut to curve just below their ears. This little girl wore her hair in the same fashion. So when she sat down on the bench between Jean and Barb, she blended right in. Three little girls with dark hair, almost like triplets. The funny part was that Dad never noticed until everyone began to snicker.

Another frequent visitor, especially in the summer months, was our friendly pastor, Father Benker. I baked bread three times a week in those days. We needed the ten loaves and the large pan of rolls to keep the family fed, bread lovers, all of them. On baking day, the family devoured all of the long pan of fresh rolls for lunch. Peanut butter and jelly on warm buns. Yum! The kids still talk about it. We discovered that our pastor also loved fresh bread one sunny summer noontime when he showed up at the back door, just as the kids sat down to eat lunch. Never one to be stiff or formal, Father Benker, eased onto the edge of the bench and reached for a hot roll. The younger children on the bench stared, open-mouthed, as he turned to them with a question.

"What do you guys put on your rolls?"

Russ spoke up. "Peanut butter and Mom's homemade jelly."

"Sounds good to me. Pass them down."

Our pastor, dressed in his black shirt and white Roman collar, dug in, munching away like the rest of the kids, rolling his eyes in delight, and washing the hot bread down with a cold glass of Kool-Aid.

That summer, I learned to set a place for our pastor, because every time I baked bread, he showed up. I swear that sweet gregarious man drove up and down the road, sniffing the air. When he smelled bread baking, his car automatically swerved into our driveway. Good memories.

Now when I know our adult children and/or grandchildren are coming to visit, I bake bread. As soon as they walk in the back door, they head for the bread drawer. Some things never change.
Cherish Every Moment.

CHAPTER 16

Learning the Lesson

Cherish every moment is not a lesson easily learned in anyone's life. Modern day living is stressful and often dangerous. When things go wrong, our first thought may be, *how can I fix this?* If things are really bad, our emotions may skip ahead to guilt or anger. Our prayer/lament may go something like this: *What did I do to deserve this, God? Haven't I been good, tried to obey your commandments, given to the church, helped at the food bank, worked with Habitat for Humanity? I don't deserve this, O God!*

But bad times come to everyone. Does God send down punishments to good people, just to see if they are paying attention? My personal belief is that bad things just happen. Sometimes they may be works of Satan to try our faith. But while we are in the throes of agony because our newborn may be dying, it is achingly difficult to trust in God's will for our lives.

When our youngest child was born, a sixth son whose birth brought our child count to ten, nothing seemed wrong at first. He was a good-sized baby, almost nine pounds, with a fuzz of hair and big blue eyes. I enjoyed the hefty weight of him as I gave him his first bottle. After a few swallows, he turned away and slept.

Nothing unusual about that, right? Newborns often fall asleep while nursing, tired out from the long labor, still a little bit fuzzy from the anesthesia, maybe. But each subsequent feeding found him blah and uninterested in food at all. The whites of his eyes looked kind of yellow. Was something wrong? Surely, such a big baby needed his formula? When I questioned the nurse, she called the doctor in for a consultation. Little Jim was given a blood test. Turned out his blood type, positive while mine is negative, caused a reaction. His skin was jaundiced and he needed a complete blood transfusion.

Oh God, oh God, oh God! What can I do? What can I do now?

Immediately, after hearing this bad news, guilt overwhelmed me. I had bad blood, it was killing my baby! Maybe I wasn't fit to be his mother? My emotions had been all over the place when we first discovered my pregnancy eight months before. Our youngest child at that time was ready for pre-school. I thought my baby days were over. Yet, another baby would soon be blessing our home. Where would we put this new little blessing? We had twelve people living in our four-bedroom home, including nine children, Dave and me, and my saintly mother-in-law. A new baby would certainly be welcome into our hearts, we knew. But the logistics of an overcrowded house seemed overwhelming. Half way through my pregnancy, we re-mortgaged our house and added three more bedrooms and a new porch onto our home. Now, our baby, little Jim might not be coming home after all. Had my negative thoughts, early in my pregnancy, somehow jinxed the future survival of our newborn?

Oh God, oh God, oh God! What can I do? What can I do now?

Dave and my mother came to the hospital and drove the sick infant to a speciality care hospital, Sisters of Mercy, in Buffalo. I stayed behind to weep and mourn for a baby who might never live to be welcomed by his nine siblings waiting anxiously at home.

Baby Jim

Hospitals kept new mothers for many days back in the late 1960's, so it was later in that week before I went home. Home with arms empty of our baby, home to a house full of disappointed, frightened children and a sad-faced grandma who fingered her rosary from morning until night. I called the hospital every day to check on the baby. Dave and I went to visit him as often as my health, weakened by a difficult childbirth and a near-nervous collapse, would allow me to take the long car ride into the city. One day I called the hospital nursery line, and due to a mix-up at the switchboard, heard the following message, "We never put through calls to the morgue, Ma'am."

Dave caught me as I screamed and fainted. In a sweat of fear, he called our doctor. Dr. Joy contacted the hospital nursery and cleared up the frightening mix-up. When the doctor called back, he gave us the good news. "You can bring that little guy home tonight, Mr. Bauer. He's doing fine."

Cherish Every Moment.

Do you think that child was cherished? Better believe it. Every person in our large and noisy household *fought* for the privilege of holding the baby, giving him his bottle, even changing his diapers! He was pampered, spoiled, given whatever he wanted within reason, and loved beyond measure. Today Jim is a big strapping guy in his early forties, good-natured, the father of two sons himself. He is the sibling who keeps the family glued together. He is the guy who always telephones his brothers and sisters, just to say hello, or to be a sympathetic ear, or to offer a broad shoulder to lean on. In other words, he is one of our family's greatest blessings.

Cherish Every Moment.

CHAPTER 17

Going Down North

Our family was complete with the birth of son, Jim. I became a working outside-the-home Mom at that time, driving a school bus during the day and working as a waitress several evenings a week. The older children were old enough to babysit for the half hour just before supper when I left for the restaurant, and Dave came home. A neighbor watched Jim for a half hour in the morning before I got home from driving the bus, and for the hour in the afternoon between the time I left for the afternoon bus run, and our high school kids got home. It was a grueling schedule for me, but it meant the bills were caught up, and we even had some money left over for luxury things, like family vacations.

Our oldest son, Dave was nineteen, out of school, and working at the Ford plant the year we bought the camping trailer. Cathy, true to her independent nature, had moved out of the house on her eighteenth birthday. Still living at home were Russ, Barb, Jean, Rose, and the four little boys, Jason, Tom, Mike and Jim. We bought a 22-foot camping trailer, self-contained with kitchen and bathroom. We built a homemade cap for our pickup truck, complete with bench seats which converted to a king-sized bed. We also included under-the-seat storage for sleeping bags and snacks.

This was before the seat-belt law which insisted children ride in properly restrained car seats, booster seats, and wear mandatory seat belts. The kids rode in the back of the truck. Dave and I, and alternating children, one at a time, rode up front in the pickup. Our first camping trip? Why, we went to Quebec! My father's ancestors raised their families in French Canada. Whenever Pop talked about going home for a visit, he always called it, Going Down North. I had made the journey several times in my childhood, once even on a train with my father.

This time our family would be driving our pickup truck and hauling a new camping trailer on a journey of several thousand miles, round trip. We had no spare tire for the trailer, no extra money, just a few hundred dollars for gas and camping fees, plus food. We had no idea of what might have gone wrong on that long trip, but we were lucky, and very blessed. Nothing serious happened to spoil the vacation of a lifetime.

Our children loved every moment. Even when it rained so hard in Montreal the truck camper leaked and all the sleeping bags got soaked. Even when Jim got soaked by a wave as he lingered too close to The Bay as the tide came in. We just built a campfire on the beach and dried his clothes, underwear and all, on a stick over the open flames.

We learned so much, all of us.

The children learned that no matter how many times they said, "Are we there yet?" we weren't there yet. The ride was long, three days of traveling in the cramped quarters of the homemade truck cap. Yet, they survived with only an occasional quarrel over who ate the last of the favorite snack, Pringles. It was usually Russ who thrust his hands into the "munchies" (as Jean called them), and devoured them before a younger sibling wrestled the prize out of his hands. To combat the loud protests over, "That greedy Russ!" he spent a lot of time up front with us.

Dave and I learned that traveling through the Matapedia Valley, between *Mont Joli*, Quebec, and Campbellton, New Brunswick, meant a bouncy ride on that notoriously rough secondary road. That meant that our cupboard doors in the trailer had better be tightly closed or we would find a real mess next meal stop. Mustard and instant coffee mixed together and smeared over the kitchen counter and floor did not lend itself well to an appetizing lunch. We learned that clothes hung in the end closet invariably leaped off the hangers whenever we rode over a bumpy road. We learned that no matter how narrow the road, nor how blind the curve or the hill ahead, some Canadian drivers insisted on passing our trailer with a loud blast of the horn. There were no double lines on Route 132, North, nor courtesy pull over lanes for slow moving units like our caravan. It was, "Look out! That car is passing us!"

God must really love the natives of French Canada because we never witnessed any wrecks, although there were plenty of close calls on the road.

Once we arrived at our destination, New Carlisle, Quebec, where Aunt Ella and Uncle Al lived, we all heaved a big sigh of relief and prayed out loud our boundless gratitude for our safe journey through the wilds of Quebec. We camped in a small camping resort just outside of town, a stone's throw from my fondly remembered *Bay de Chaleur*. Every breath we took invited the salty sting of ocean air into our lungs. It even followed us to our dreams.

The first morning, we all were awakened by the haunting call of seabirds. The children called them Canadian roosters. The screeches and calls of those beautiful white and black birds took me back in time to a childhood visit when my cousin Jean and I rolled down the hill by our aunt's cottage by the sea. I woke up smiling, grateful and happy that my children could also experience the sights, sounds, and delightful smells that my ancestors experienced down through the ages. We visited the beach every day.

The kids learned that marshmallows roasted over a campfire of driftwood from the ocean tasted salty. Dave learned that sometimes the water pressure in a camping ground is so high it blasts the hose off the commode pipe. We learned that LaBatts Canadian beer is so strong, drinking a half bottle would make us slide out of our lawn chairs. We started calling that brand, La Blatts. Still do. We learned that Aunt Ella's ginger cookies, if they are baked too long, have a new name. Jim called them Ginger Blacks. But we ate every one!

Rose knew some French from her high school language class and that helped a great deal, especially when dealing with small stores whose owners did not speak English. Dave learned that if a Frenchman does not understand when you ask for a bag of ice, repeating the request in a louder voice does not make the shopkeeper understand at all. We all learned French to English place names. *Trois Rivera* in French translates to Three Rivers. *Bay de Chaleur* means Bay of Heat in English. We learned other vital French words. *Arrett* on a sign means Stop! *Est* is east, *Qest* is west. *Lave'* means wash or bathe. *Monsieur* on a public restroom door means Mens' Room. *Mademoiselle* is the Ladies' Room. It was a long way from our usual camping experiences in the States, where Buck and Doe marked the public facilities.

Jim, five years old at that time, was our goodwill ambassador. Whenever a new family moved into the campground, little Jim always went over to greet the new people.

"Do you speak, En-ga-lish?" he asked. His charming way, and big smile, always earned him a treat of some kind, such as a homemade cookie or a croissant.

Cherish Every Moment!

CHAPTER 18

❧

The Sea Change

But the most important lesson Dave and I experienced on our vacation trip to Quebec was the Sea Change. We borrowed my Uncle Al's small aluminum flat-bottomed boat to go fishing on The Bay. It had an outboard motor that Dave and Al had worked on for an entire day, before it finally roared to life. First the guys took a sixty mile round trip to New Richmond to buy a thirty cent O ring part for the outboard motor. Uncle Al thought Dave was a genius mechanic because no one in that area knew how to fix anything with a motor, especially car motors. Al was so impressed by Dave's knowledge and skill, he offered to set him up in his own business. He wanted us to move to Canada and live in New Carlisle. It was tempting, but we had so many ties in the USA, Dave had to turn him down.

To thank Dave for fixing the outboard motor, Uncle Al loaned us the boat.

We towed the boat to the Butter-factory Beach. Somewhere in the distant past, my ancestors owned a butter factory. The factory was long gone now, but the beach still remained, a beautiful spot, with pink quartz rocks and red sand. We took along a picnic

lunch and enjoyed High Tea on the Butter-factory Beach. The
kids loved it. They spent the afternoon collecting shells, driftwood in interesting shapes, and pink rocks.

Meanwhile Dave and I went fishing in the boat.

Dave had caught the fishing bug earlier that visit when my
cousin Goldie took us both out on the Bay to fish for cod. We
needed to buy Visitor's licenses first, because fishing the Bay is
strictly regulated by the Provincial Government. The cost was
small, less than five dollars. Goldie, as a commercial fisherman,
could accompany us, but was not allowed to sell any fish we might
catch. We rode in my cousin's large fishing boat, a wooden boat
with a wide beam and a big inboard motor. We really lucked-out
that time because we caught a boat full of cod, enough to feed our
family for a week, plus plenty more to give away. Now, on our
own in Al's boat, we tried again to catch some fish.

The Bay was calm as we started out (Uncle Al said, "The Bay is
cam."). The children waved as the little outboard motor carried our
small craft away from the beach. With Dave at the helm, we putt-
putted our way across the clear water. I looked down through the
clear water and watched darting minnows, almost invisible jelly-
fish and silver herring slide beneath the bow of the boat. The sound
of the motor droning on made me sleepy. I almost drifted off for a
nap before Dave decided to drop anchor. I awoke with a start.

"We're out kind of far, aren't we, Dave?"

"Just a couple of miles, I think."

I stared toward the shoreline, a long way off, it seemed to me.
Too far by far! The children looked ant-like, toy figures walking
up and down the shore, shading their eyes, and staring out to sea.

"Look!" Dave said and pointed. "A blue whale."

Sure enough, maybe a hundred yards further out to sea, a
large sea mammal rose up through the waves and splashed down
again. *Wow!*

Behind me Dave let out a soft oath.

"What? Something wrong?"

"The anchor won't hold. We must be too deep."

"Dave, we are out too far."

"Nah, just bait your hook. Want to catch some fish, don't you?"

I opened my mouth to reply when something physical and very weird took my breath away. It is difficult to describe the sensation in mere words. I have a pet theory that God holds us in the palm of his hands. And when we experience something very frightening, something traumatic, it feels as if our loving Creator opens his hands and just lets us slide away from the safety of God's embrace. Now, at sea in a tiny boat, like the Apostles when Jesus fell asleep in their fishing boat, I experienced a terrorizing moment of falling through space, of helpless vertigo.

Sea Change.

* * *

David

I stared at my wife. Her face grew very white. *What just happened?* My stomach yawned open and started jumping around. It felt the same as the time Cecile talked me into riding the double Ferris Wheel at the Erie County Fair. As soon as we went over the top, my heart dropped into my belly. I felt like up-chucking my lunch. Now, sitting in a little boat in the big wide ocean, I felt just as scared and unsettled. Something caught my eye. I pointed off to the right. She turned to stare. The level of ocean water at that point looked five feet taller than the spot where we sat in Uncle Al's aluminum boat.

"What on earth?" I said. My voice shook

"The tide is changing," she said. "Better get back to shore. Now!"

* * *

Cecile

Without another word, Dave turned to start the outboard motor. I hauled anchor rope quickly, hand over hand, careful not to wrap the rope around our feet. If the boat swamped, the anchor rope would drag us down to the depths of the sea. The nine-horsepower outboard motor roared to life. Dave pointed the nose of the boat toward the distant shore. We headed in.

Our return trip to the beach seemed to take twice as long as the trip out. The motor kept coughing as the growing swells of ocean waves took us up, up, up, and then down into the steep troughs. Each time we topped the ever-higher waves, the motor prop rose out of the water and sputtered. We prayed, oh how we prayed, to reach the safety of shore and our beloved waiting children. Like the frightened fishermen who would become Jesus' fearless Apostles, I prayed.

"Lord, does it not matter to you that we are going to drown?" Mark 4:38

Putt-putt, up the tall waves. Sputter. Down into the deep troughs of the sea. Putt-putt, sputter. Seawater splashed into the boat. I bailed it out with a small coffee can. Putt-putt, sputter. We prayed.

I thought of my grandfather, Jimmy Ramier (pronounced *Ram-Yay* by the French), who rowed his flat bottomed wooden boat out into the ocean every day in order to catch fish and feed his family. As had his ancestors and mine. Not once, in the long history of family fishermen, had any of them drowned at sea. But they could read the sky and the tides. Not like Dave and me, Yanks from the States who put our lives at risk so foolishly.

Putt-putt, up the tall waves. Sputter, down into the deep troughs of the sea. Putt-putt, sputter. Slowly, oh so slowly, our children's welcoming faces drew nearer. The sharp scrape as the bottom of the boat slid onto the gravel of the shore never sounded so good. Both of us stepped carefully out of the boat, on legs that trembled and shook, and hugged our children tight.

"Did you catch any fish?" Jim asked. He wondered why we laughed so much.

The next day, when we again took the boat out, the motor refused to start at all. The *what ifs* haunted the rest of our vacation. *What if the motor had refused to start while we were two miles out in the ocean and the tide changed? What if the boat swamped by the big waves? What if we drowned out there?* I can float for hours but Dave swims like a rock, straight to the bottom. *What if we never came back to our family?*

Thank you, God, for keeping us safe in the palm of your hand.

We returned the boat to Uncle Al and parked it in his garage. As far as I know, he never took that boat out again.

Cherish Every Moment!

❧❀❧

CHAPTER 19

Boil *a* Kettle

While on the same Canadian vacation trip, we stopped in New Brunswick to visit Aunt Jean and Uncle Dave. Jean was one of my favorite aunts, so gentle and kind, yet full of fun. She was always up for an adventure. Uncle Dave had retired from the Canadian National Railroad on a disability for a serious back injury. To keep busy during the long, northern winters, this tall virile man of Scottish descent often sat and did needlepoint. His finely worked rendition of a vase of roses beautified the parlor of their small home in Tidehead, New Brunswick.

During the warmer months, Uncle Dave built canoes. Not your ordinary plastic or aluminum canoe, but lovingly crafted twenty-foot-long wooden boats capable of supporting an outboard motor on one end. He built them in his basement, then took out part of a wall in order to bring the large boats outside. While we were there in the summer of 1973, Uncle Dave took us across the *Restigouche* River to a nearby island, to have a picnic supper. It took three trips to carry all of our family, plus the food Aunt Jean so lovingly prepared ahead of time.

She stepped out of the canoe with a big smile, looked around briefly, nodded her approval and said, "Time to boil a kettle."

This, we Yanks learned, was Canadian-speak for, "Let's build a campfire, so we can hang a pot of water over the flames. When the water boils, we can make tea."

Our sons gathered wood for the campfire, and the men made the fire. We women, Aunt Jean and me, and our three daughters, Barb, Jean Marie and Rose, spread a tablecloth on the ground, unpacked the picnic basket, and arranged the lavish spread of goodies.

"Aunt Jean, you outdid yourself," I said and gave her a hug.

She blushed and looked pleased. "It's just picnic food," she said.

Rose peeked under the lid of a steaming pot. Fragrant scents of chicken and sage wafted into the crisp air.

"What is this?" she said, nibbling on a tiny piece of something good.

"It's chicken and rice, Child," Aunt Jean said, smiling.

"Rice! Yuck!" Rose said. But she snuck out another piece of rice to taste. "Not too shabby," she said, and licked her fingers.

"Rose!" I said, "Don't be so rude!" I turned to apologize to my generous aunt. "'Not too shabby' in teen-talk means it tastes delicious, Aunt Jean."

She didn't seem to be offended by my daughter's lack of manners. In fact, Aunt Jean was laughing as she watched the expression on my bold daughter's face. Rose licked her fingers again.

"Want the recipe, Rose?"

My youngest daughter, thank God, smiled and nodded. "Sure would. This is good!"

Needless to say, chicken and rice became a family favorite from that day on. Rose often makes it for her own family now.

Cherish Every Moment!

CHAPTER 20

❧

Tommy Tippy
and Fishing for Pike

When our children were small, we owned a small plastic cup with a rounded bottom. A forerunner of today's sippy-cups, the cup helped wean our toddlers from bottle to cup. The cup, named Tommy-Tippy, had a cover. If the toddler's fingers slipped and the cup fell, it always landed right-side up without spilling any milk.

During our camping years, after our visit with Uncle Dave and his marvelous canoes, we decided to buy an aluminum canoe for fishing. Given the instability of canoes in general, we named our canoe Tommy Tippy. The canoe took hard use from our large family. Each of the children learned to paddle and maneuver around Rainbow Lake, our favorite local campground. We owned life jackets in every size. Despite the fact that all of our children were skilled swimmers, we strictly enforced the wear-the-jacket-or-stay-out-of-the-canoe rule. Good thing, because many of our more reckless boys often hit the shallow water of the man-made lake. *Splash! Boy overboard.* The canoe, true to its name, always righted itself.

One weekend, Dave and I decided to take a little glide around the lake. We carried the canoe down to one of the many docks provided for the campers and dropped it into the water. I held onto the lead rope, while Dave stepped into the boat. Or tried to step into the boat. Even though I held tight to the rope attached to the front of the canoe, the back of the boat had a mind of its own. Just as Dave planted one foot into the center of the boat, it began to slide sideways. He ended up doing an impossible-to-balance split, one leg in the boat, the other one on the dock. *Splash, man in the water!*

He wasn't too happy about it, especially since I laughed so hard, but he wore old shoes and it didn't really matter. We did get our romantic, if wet-footed, canoe ride anyway.

Next trip out with the canoe, he wasn't so lucky.

We had taken the camper and the canoe up to the Thousand Islands along the St. Lawrence River. Our neighbors, Aggie and Bob, had a summer home up there and had invited us to visit them.

"The fishing is great, Dave," Bob promised. "Northern Pike and Bass, great fun!"

The first fishing trip, we went on Bob's big boat with the in-board motor. We fished for Large-mouthed Bass, and managed to catch enough for supper. The Bass are fun to land, they put up a challenging fight on the end of the line.

I enjoy fishing. It is the action of casting out and reeling in that makes it fun for me. It doesn't really matter whether I catch anything or not. I enjoy the casting! Dave just wanted to catch fish.

We were standing, facing opposite sides of the boat. Dave faced west, Bob and I faced east. I kept casting out, getting more and more ambitious, trying to see how far out I could land the hook and sinker.

Suddenly, behind me, Dave yelped. "Hey!"

"What?" I said, turning my head.

"That last cast of yours came pretty close to my head! I felt the hook zip passed my ear!"

"Oops! Sorry," I said. But I hid a grin.

Bob burst out laughing. He has a deep, infectious laugh that invites anyone nearby to join in. Even Dave laughed when Bob began to chuckle. I turned back to my casting and concentrated on keeping my flying fishing hook away from my husband's head. Moments later, Dave yelped again.

"What? My hook didn't come near you!"

Bob roared with laughter. "Sorry, Dave! My hook tore loose. Did it catch you on the backlash?"

"No! Your sinker hit me on top of the head."

Bob laughed so hard he almost dropped his fishing pole. "Must be pick-on-Dave night," he said, choking. He had to swipe tears out of his eyes.

Dave said, "I should have brought along my hard hat from work, maybe?"

But even a hard hat could not have saved Dave the next day.

This time we decided to take our own canoe fishing on French Creek. We were hoping to catch some elusive Northern Pike. The creek had a pretty good current as it flowed into the river, so Bob offered to tow us in our canoe up the creek about a mile. We could then drift back, dragging a short line with a special Pike lure. We used short poles, because casting out was not an option in our stability challenged Tommy-Tippy.

After Bob turned the tow rope lose, he went up the creek a bit and dropped anchor. We settled down to drift along, trying to catch some Pike. My line jerked.

"Got one," I said, excited, and reeled it in.

It was well over the minimum limit of fourteen inches. Dave

leaned over a bit to scoop it up with our short-handled net. He left it in the net and picked up his fishing pole. "My turn to catch one," he said.

We drifted for a bit, but no more Pike nibbled on our lines.

"Let's go back to where you caught that one," Dave said, and made a sudden lunge to pick up the oars. Uh oh!

Splash! Two people in the water!

I came up sputtering. Dave stood a few feet from me, up to his shoulders in creek water. Green tendrils of sea grass hung from his hat. Relieved that the water was not deep enough to drown him, I made a grab for the fishing net floating past. It still held the Pike I had caught minutes before.

"I got my fish!" I said.

Dave grabbed the other fishing equipment floating around. True to its name, Tommy-Tippy had righted itself. I managed to grab the lead rope and hang on. We tossed our belonging, including my big fish, into the boat. A few yards away, Bob had witnessed the whole thing. He turned his back, shoulders hunched as he struggled to start the big boat and give us a tow back to the cabin. Bob seemed to take a long time to start his boat. I realized by the strangled sounds coming from him, and his shaking shoulders, that he was struggling not to laugh out loud.

Somehow we managed to climb back into our canoe and begin the inglorious ride back French Creek to Bob's summer home. We looked like two creatures from a drowned lagoon, wet moss hanging from our bodies, our clothing soaked, even our hats damp and dripping.

At one point I turned to Dave. "Thank God the creek wasn't too deep," I said.

"But I'm wearing my Sunday shoes," he protested.

"Well Dave, I guess they are your Monday shoes now," I said and burst out laughing.

When we arrived back at the cabin, Aggie ran for her camera. When we went into our camping trailer to change into dry clothing, we discovered sea grass had invaded every part of our clothing, including our underwear. But we still had my fish, the elusive Northern Pike. It remains the only Pike I have every hooked. But oh, the sweet and funny memories of Tommy-Tippy, our unpredictable canoe.

Cherish Every Moment!

CHAPTER 21

Fiɞhing Poleɞ,
Loveɒ anɒ Loɞt

Over the years of our long marriage, we have purchased at least a dozen fishing poles. They made an inexpensive and popular birthday gift for those children born in the summer months, Dave Jr., Cathy, Jean, Tom, Mike and Jim. In those days, a complete fishing rig: pole, reel, line and accessories, cost less than five dollars. Most of the children loved to fish. Jean, especially, seemed born to the sport.

Although, the first time Jean went fishing as a toddler, she did put up quite a protest. My middle sister, Betty and her husband, Len, came out to visit one fine summer's day. They brought along their fishing gear, an entire metal box full of lures, hooks, bobbers, and extra line. Their goal? To expose our as then ignorant children to the joys of fishing.

Len strolled into the woods across the road and returned with a bundle of flexible sticks, fishing rods in the rough, so to speak. Betty helped fasten fiberglass fishing line to each stick. Len tied on small hooks and bobbers.

"Ready to go fishing, Kids?"

"Yes!"

They were not sure what *going fishing* meant, but they were always up for an adventure.

After lunch Betty and Len set out with the five oldest children, Davy, Cathy, Russ, Barb and Jean, then barely two years old. They drove the car filled with excited amateur fisher-children to a nearby creek called Kromer's Mill. I waved good-bye with baby Rose in my arms. As soon as the car left the end of the driveway, Rose and I went down for a nap.

Later that day, the fisher people returned, soaked, exhausted (Betty and Len), and so hyped up they could barely contain themselves (the children, that is). A cluster of muddy little children with high, excited voices burst into the kitchen. They all talked at once. Trying to sort through the shrill babble, I heard one strong theme: *Jean caught a fish!*

Behind them in the doorway, Betty grinned through her fatigue. Len's lips turned down in that familiar upside down smile. He chuckled.

"Jean caught a fish all right," he said.

Betty giggled. "You should have seen her, Sis. It was priceless!"

I shooed the older kids toward the bathroom for a clean up and picked up Jean. She laid her little head on my shoulder and heaved a big sigh.

"Did you catch a fish, Jeannie?"

She nodded and scrubbed at her eyes. I could feel her fatigue as she slumped against me.

"How exciting!" I said.

We moved toward the bathroom to wash her up so she could take a much-needed nap.

"Exciting is right," Len said. "You should have seen her. As soon as she hooked the fish, she screamed."

He held his ears. "Never knew kids could scream that loud. Wow!"

Betty giggled and mimicked Jean's excitement. She waved an invisible fishing pole up and down. "Ahhhhhh! Eeeeeee!"

Len added. "She was trying to shake the fish off the line."

Jean squirmed in my arms. "No fish! No fish on my string," she said.

Despite this early trauma, Jean grew to enjoy fishing, a love of the sport that continues to this day. When we lived in California, Jean and her family invited us to go camping to Bear Lake, a famous fishing spot in the Sacramento area. It turned out to be a fun weekend, even if I did lose my favorite fishing pole.

My very favorite fishing pole was a fiberglass one originally given to son Tom as a birthday gift. When he grew up and left home to move to California, he left this pole behind. I loved the flexible feel of it, the way I could cast way out over the water with just a flick of the wrist. Many times, while out camping with the remnants of our family, I spent hours just casting out and reeling in. Didn't matter to me whether I caught a fish or not. It calmed and relaxed me to just cast out and reel in. When we retired and moved west, my favorite fishing pole went along.

The first morning at Bear Lake, I hustled to assemble my fishing gear. It seemed a short walk to the edge of the water. Finding an empty spot near water's edge, I cast out and reeled in. The sun was bright, the water calm, and I was fishing. Ah, paradise! Around me other fishermen reeled in fat trout. I cast out and reeled in, unconcerned about catching anything other than the satisfaction that comes from relaxing at water's edge.

Opps! My line snagged on something. I wiggled the pole, trying to shake the line loose. The harder I shook the pole, the tougher the hook dug into some underwater snag.

Snap! Oh no!

The pole in my hand, my very favorite fishing pole for casting out and reeling in, snapped in two. I stared at the short piece of handle in my hand, reel attached, line trailing into the lake. A desperate sorrow washed over me. My favorite pole! Broken! No more casting out and reeling in.

Angry and disappointed, I flung the rest of the fishing gear into the lake.

"You want it, you got it," I said and stalked away.

My fishing days are over.

That marked the last time I actually went fishing.

A few years before that I had lost another favorite pole. This one was very short, a beginner's rod for children. The children outgrew it, but it worked perfectly for fishing out of a boat. Dave and I were the guests of Jim's father-in-law, Dick, who owned a small aluminum boat. He took us out on Lake Erie to try for Big-mouthed Bass. This is a fine fighting fish, fun to hook and reel in, tasty on the table. Dick and Dave sat at opposite ends of the boat, I sat in the middle seat, facing Dave. We had good luck hooking fish that day. Too bad so many of them were toss-back fish. All of us hooked our share of Groupers, a garbage fish, which we un-hooked and tossed back. Behind me Dick made a remark.

"Ever think we might all be catching and releasing the same Grouper?"

We laughed as Dave reeled in yet another garbage fish. They are slimy and wiggly. He struggled to take the hook out of the fish's mouth. I reached out for the fish.

"Here, let me do it," I said.

I clamped my fishing pole between my thighs to keep it safe while I wrestled with the slippery fish.

Zip! My fishing pole flew out from between my legs and sailed out into the lake.

"Whoa!" Dick said.

Dick tried to retrieve my pole by casting out in the direction that it had taken when it flew out of the boat. No luck.

"Gone with the wind," I said and laughed.

Might as well laugh, since I lack the ability to walk on water. Ah fishing, I miss it.

Cherish Every Moment.

❧❀❧

CHAPTER 22

The Oasis

That first camping trip to Quebec spoiled us with its absence of problems. We thought all camping trips would be so carefree. *Wrong!*

A few summers after that, we decided to travel west on a grand tour of National Parks. We wanted to see the Grand Canyon, the Carlsbad Caverns, and other attractions out west. We had three weeks of vacation and a few hundred dollars for gas and camping fees. What could go wrong?

Grand Canyon was awesome, the Painted Desert so beautiful, but the Petrified Forest a disappointment. No forest at all, nothing but level desert, parched, dry and nothing much to see. *Hmmm. Maybe this is why the Chosen people of God got so discouraged in the Sinai desert? Imagine, forty years spent wandering in this desert heat and desolation.* My spirits sagged.

We were all pretty cranky that day. A photograph taken on that occasion showed our sour-spirited group with everyone frowning. Time for a break from the heat.

Carlsbad Caverns seemed so cool the next day. Well worth the extra gasoline to drive down to New Mexico. We camped at a really nice place with a swimming pool. The kids loved it and wanted to stay extra days there.

"Sorry, kids. Money is growing short. Time to head home."

We were driving through Texas when the stiff side wind blew the cover off one of our roof vents. If we hit rain on the way home, the camping trailer would suck up the rain and be flooded. That meant we had to stop at the next Recreational Vehicle dealer and buy a replacement vent cover.

Texas in the summertime. Hot 100-degree winds blowing across the metal roof of our trailer as Dave struggled to replace the vent cover. He had only two screwdrivers, not the proper tools to install the cover whose holes were in the wrong places. He used one of his work shoes as a hammer, and the oldest screwdriver to punch holes into the metal. As he worked, I made supper in the trailer.

Cooking smells from the hot dogs wafted up through the open vent and attracted hoards of flies. Dave cussed and swatted flies, swiping away the sweat running into his eyes, as he struggled to install the stubborn vent cover. Finally he finished. Flushed and sweaty, he descended into the trailer, gobbled up his supper and climbed back behind the wheel of our pickup truck. We had no air conditioning in the truck, but the breeze from the open window soon cooled him off.

"We better make as much time as we can," he said. "Need to get home before Saturday so we can cash my paycheck."

On those long camping trips, Dave did all the driving. I offered to help drive, but he didn't trust my lack of experience hauling a trailer. I felt bad for him, knowing how tired he was from his hours behind the wheel, fighting the stiff winds of Texas, battling fatigue as we headed northeast to our New York State home.

That night, we were on the road until almost midnight before Dave pulled over in a rest stop near Lubbock. No facilities, no water or restrooms, just a pull-off in the middle of the dark Texas night. As we prepared to crash in the trailer for the night, a Texas Ranger pulled along side our rig and looked us over.

"You-all staying here for the night?" he asked.

We nodded, too exhausted to say much. "We've been driving all day up from New Mexico," I said and sighed. "We just need some sleep before we go on."

"That's fine, Ma'am. Just as long as you don't put up a tent or try to camp on the grass."

"Yes Sir," I said. "We all sleep in the trailer."

He smiled and left soon after, wishing us a good trip.

The next morning I woke up first. Our trailer battery had died the day before. That meant the refrigerator didn't work. We had to toss out spoiled food, milk, mayonnaise, and slimy lunch meat. No battery power also meant no water could be pumped from our in-trailer reservoir. No water to make instant coffee, no water to stir up milk using the box of powdered milk in our emergency supply, no water to make instant orange juice. Not even a trickle of water to wash my face. What would be have for breakfast? We certainly had no extra cash to eat breakfast at a diner, even if we could find a restaurant cheap enough for our hoard of hungry people. I stared out the trailer screen door at the expanse of green grass surrounding the rest area

What to do? Oh God, where are you this beautiful Texas morning?

Whoosh! The sprinklers, which kept the grass green, popped up and began their revolving job of hydration. Cool mists rose from the dampening lawn.

Thanks, God!

Grabbing up the empty coffee pot, I hustled out to the nearest sprinkler and waited for it to point my way. Not easy filling the pot when the high pressure splashed water into the pot and out again just as fast. Did get a nice cool shower though, since it took me three trips to fill enough containers for breakfast. By the time the kids awoke, breakfast cereal and nice cold instant milk awaited their eager spoons. I lit the gas stove with a kitchen match and heated water for coffee. Dave and I enjoyed our breakfast before heading down the road again. Later that day, we stopped at a rest stop in Oklahoma to clean up. I washed my hair using cold water from the ladies' room.

Despite the perils of that long trip, we did arrive home in time to cash Dave's waiting paycheck. Good thing, because we were all tired, dirty and practically starved. That night, for supper, we bought fried chicken from the fish store in Eden and enjoyed every bite.

Cherish Every Moment.

CHAPTER 23

Tom, Help!

Time, as time does, flew past. Our family, on the cusp of a sea change during those wonderful camping years, had dwindled down to the three youngest sons at home, and Rose living in the upstairs apartment. The year was 1980 and I bought a new car. Rose needed a car so we gave her my 1974 Nova. But before the paperwork came through from DMV, the boys used the old car for one more job.

Our driveway had always been gravel. In fact the children used to make roads and play cars in the driveway when they were little. Because they all were so close in age, they played quite well together. Never at a loss for playmates, they planned roadways through the gravel, and shoved their various little metal toy cars and trucks in endless games of their own inventions. As they got older, they made bicycle ramps and obstacle courses (training for their eventual graduation to driving real cars). Whatever their driveway games, they came to a sudden screeching halt every summer afternoon at 4:30. From my vantage point in the kitchen, I would open the window and yell out to those busy little people, "Dad will be home soon. Get the rakes."

Groans went up from the peanut gallery. But they knew Dad would pitch a fit if *his* driveway was, "All torn up," when he arrived home for supper. The younger children would gather up the toy cars or shove the bicycles into the shed. The older kids grabbed the rakes and groaned as they destroyed their carefully constructed interstate exchanges.

But that was long ago. The older children had grown up and moved away. Only Tom, 18, Mike, 16, and Jim, 12 still lived at home. Too old now to play in the driveway with toy cars. But that didn't stop them from playing in the driveway with a real car.

The gravel driveway, a thin layer of crushed stone over hard-packed dirt, had a habit of losing its gravel topping. The small stones were flung off into the lawn by car tires when someone was in a hurry to go somewhere. The gravel was scraped off in the winter by snow shovels, and later, blown off the driveway by the walk-behind snow thrower. Each spring, bare spots and muddy ruts made the driveway messy. Keeping the mud out of the house became an endless chore. Each spring, as soon as the mud stopped freezing and heaving with lingering winter weather, I called our local supplier for another load of gravel to top off our driveway.

But before we ordered more gravel, the driveway needed to be scraped smooth. This was accomplished by dragging a set of old bed springs across the rough spots to smooth out the deeper ruts. That way, the new gravel would lay nice and smooth, and maybe (*please God?*), this time it might stick around longer.

Tom and Mike were assigned the task of dragging the driveway smooth. They did this by tying a tow rope on one end of our driveway-scraping tool, the bare bedsprings, and attaching the rope to the back bumper of my old car, the Nova. Tom drove. Mike sat on the back bumper and kept his feet on the springs to keep them close to the driveway instead of bouncing around and leaping over the ruts.

They started off slowly. Tom drove up the driveway to the road. Mike rode on the bumper. At the entrance of the driveway, on the public road, Mike got off, picked up the springs as Tom backed up. As soon as the car was once more on the driveway, Mike climbed back on the bumper. The second trip down the driveway was a little faster. Mike ya-hooed as the springs leaped up over a deep rut, but he kept control of the bouncing springs.

The third trip was even faster, too fast by far. Suddenly the old bedsprings sprang to life! It bounced so high, it rose off the driveway and flipped over. Mike hung on as the springs did a loop-the-loop. Now Mike was under the springs and being dragged down the driveway, through the muddy ruts toward the road. Did his life flash before his eyes? Could be, because he began to howl.

"Tommmmmmmm! Help!"

Tom, our always-serious son, stopped the car at the end of the driveway. With an exasperated expression on his face, he unbuckled the seatbelt, and opened the door. Watching from the kitchen window I could read his thoughts. *"Now what has that screw-up brother done?"*

When he stepped to the back of the car, Tom's face got very red as he struggled hard not to laugh.

Mike had, and still has, a wicked temper. Tom knew that if he laughed out loud, it would bring on a king-sized tantrum from his younger brother. Mike lay under the bedsprings, his face and glasses splattered with mud. His jeans and his favorite denim jacket were filthy. His only belt, a wide Western belt Mike was very proud of, was torn in two. Tom's face got redder.

"Mike? What the heck?"

"Quit laughing," Mike roared. "Just get this stupid thing off of me!"

While the boys struggled to untangle the mess of rope, springs and trapped victim, I hustled to the basement to start the washer.

Sure enough, moments later Mike stomped down the cellar steps. Without a word he handed me his denim jacket. Without laughing out loud (though it was really tough to keep a straight face), I pointed at his filthy jeans.

"Want those washed, too, Mike?" I said in a strangled voice.

He went behind the furnace and peeled off his jeans. I kept my back turned to protect his boyish modesty (and to hide my laughter). Behind me I heard him muttering.

"My favorite jeans! My coat! And it broke my belt!"

From the top of the basement steps Tom hooted. "Bad day for Michael Mouse?"

"Don't call me that! And quit laughing!"

Mike tore up the steps, roaring, bare legs flying. His jockey shorts needed washing too, but I never had a chance to tell him. Intent on catching Tom, Mike took off after his brother. Both boys flew out the back door. Ah me, the adventures of raising boys! I laughed so hard I could hardly pour the detergent.

Need I say it?

Cherish Every Moment.

CHAPTER 24

Teaching Drivers' Ed, the Home Edition

The only drawback to having a large family is those sweet little toddlers have a way of growing up and becoming teenagers. Teenagers, as in, *"Mom, when can I get my learner's permit?"*

Nothing strikes terror into my heart like the prospect of taking a sixteen year old hot-shot who knows everything (except how to keep my car under control), out for his or her first driving lesson. The teens were all pretty sharp when it came to acing the written test. Not one failed that part of the learner's permit application. It helped that our school district, Eden Central, taught Driver's Ed as an elective course. Twenty weeks of instruction: ten weeks on the paper work, plus using a driving simulator (think one of those hot-rod driving games you encounter at the supermarket entrance-way). Once the teens had their learner's permit, then the second half of the course, the actual road experience began. Parents were encouraged to take their novice drivers on practice runs also, of course. And that is when my brown hair turned gray (could be a Crystal Gail song).

Davy Ravy had grown up craving a motorcycle. He worked with me at Holiday Inn, washing dishes, to save enough money for a small cycle. By age fifteen, he had wheels and he burned up the farmers' fields and the dirt roads nearby, roaring along, singing a song. The kid was never happier than when he was on wheels. But driving a dirt bike across the fields is vastly different than driving Mom's car down the public highway, a whole 'nother world, and a lot scarier, for me anyway.

The boy suffered from over-confidence. One arm out the window, radio blasting, he cruised along as if he owned the road.

"Davy! Slow down! Davy, put both hands on the wheel! Davy, you are following too close to that truck. *David! Stop!*"

He laughed. "Don't worry, Mom. I know what I am doing. I won't wreck your car."

At that point I was less worried about wrecking my car, than I was of wrecking my health. My heart pounded as wildly as if I was having a heart seizure.

Dare I mention that he passed his official road test on the first try?

Now, Cathy was a girl after my own heart. She had no designs on road privileges until she was almost eighteen. Content to let her father or me drive her back and forth to her after-school job, she seemed far too nervous to even apply for a learner's permit. But already she spoke about being on her own. I couldn't release her into the cold cruel world unless she at least owned a driver's license!

Finally, I thought of an easy way to get her behind the wheel, something harmless, something she would be comfortable with. While getting ready for my job at the Inn one afternoon, I called Cathy into the bedroom and handed her the keys to my car.

"Cathy? Be a sweetheart and bring my car to the back door?"

"But, Mom! What if I hit something?"

"There is nothing between the garage and the back door for you to hit."

"But, Mom? I don't know ..." She stared at the keys in her hand as if they might spring to life and bite her.

I sighed. "Ask Davy to go with you."

Reluctantly, she turned and went down the hallway to her older brother's room. I heard his teasing laughter as she made her request.

"Be right there, Cath. Meet you in the garage. I have to get something, first."

I glanced out the hall door just in time to see him pull on his motorcycle helmet.

"Now I'm ready," he said and buckled the chin strap.

I heard the two of them laughing hysterically as they walked together to the garage.

Despite her brother's lack of confidence in her driving ability, Cathy did get her license. But not without certain mishaps. One evening, as her father drove her home from work, he pulled over at the end of our country road to switch drivers. It was about four miles to our house, a nice little practice jaunt for our insecure daughter. He drove my 1966 Impala Super Sport, a wonderful car. It had bucket seats, lush leather upholstery, and a central console with an automatic shifter in it. Because it was a two-door sedan, the doors were extra wide to allow people to climb into the back seat. Dave called those doors, *pneumonia holes*, since they let in so much cold air in the winter time.

"Here you go, Cathy. Your turn to drive."

He set the gear shift into Park, then climbed out and walked around to get in the passenger side. Cathy had left her door open after she climbed out to switch drivers. Dave had one foot in the car when Cathy plunged the gear shift into Drive and hit the gas.

"Wait-wait-*wait!*" Dave yelped. "I'm not in the car yet!"

"Oh, sorry Dad," she said and shoved the gear shift into Park.

Dave, half in and half out of that big passenger door, was flung forward into the space between door frame and wide open door. *"Cathy!"* he yelled. "Are you trying to kill me?"

Cathy and I share an unfortunate habit. When we are nervous, we giggle, and giggle and *giggle*, until our faces grow red from embarrassment. She turned to her father.

"Dad, maybe you should drive?"

Dave had finally made it into the car and slammed shut the pneumonia hole. He braced himself against the dash and drew a deep calming breath. His hands shook a little, but he waved toward the road.

"Go ahead, Cathy. Just take it slow, OK?"

So by leaps and stutters, they did get home. Dave said it was the longest four miles he ever endured. After that experience, Dave confined himself to the role of teacher of parallel-parking, the last learning step before the driver's road test.

When the novice driver had enough driving time under his or her seat belt, and just before the highly anticipated and greatly feared *road test*, Dave took out the new driver to teach the basics of parallel parking. At first they used to go into the nearest town with curbs bordering the streets. But many people, seeing their parked cars about to be endangered by a new-to-the-drill parking novice, would race out of their homes to move their cars out of danger. You can't teach a teen how to pull up beside a parked car, twist the steering wheel one way, then crank it the other way as they slowly backed into an empty slot, when there was no car parked there in the first place. Dave would come home disgruntled and grumpy, the parking lesson untaught, the novice driver clueless as how to parallel park.

"How can I pass my road test now?" the teens would complain, throwing their hands into the air in an unconscious imitation of Dad's disgust.

Finally we came up with a solution. Since we had so many children, they could pretend they were parked vehicles! We even had a private curb to aim for, down at the high school!

So we loaded up the car with willing automobile stand-ins, and took the whole raucous crew to the high school parking lot. The younger kids knew their time would come to learn to park. This was just a way to pay ahead, to make brownie points with Dad.

First Dave pulled up to the curb and unloaded all the children except the new driver. Using the car as a measure point, the younger kids took up positions at the front and back. If there were enough brave volunteers, they made a human line to represent the side of a parked car. Dad switched places with the apprentice driver. Under Dave's calm prodding the teen swung out and pulled along side the line of siblings, who were holding hands and jeering just to make things interesting.

"OK now, just back up slowly, twist the steering wheel to the right, slowly now."

Dave stuck his head out the window. "Which one of you ya-hoos is the back tire?"

When the wheel-man raised his hand, Dave turned to the driver. "Now when your front tires pass the back wheels of the car, see, it's Tom this time, then crank the steering wheel the other way. Slowly now."

While all this was happening, the novice driver was sweating bullets. The car had the jimmy jumps as the driver's foot went from gas pedal to brake as he or she struggled to remember which way to crank the wheel, at the same time watching out that they didn't run over one of the younger children.

"Not bad," Dave would say as the car tilted to one side because the tire was up on the curb. "Let's try that again." He had the patience of Job. Thanks to his careful teaching, all the children ended up with their driver's license.

Of course, I helped. Road experience was left to me by default. Did I mention that my hair turned gray in my early thirties? Ten children means a lot of road terror along the way. But I am grateful that the off-road joy ride that Jean took happened in the Driver's Ed car and not mine!

It happened in the winter time, an icy day. Seriously, I think the Driver Ed teacher should have known better than to take out a group of high school kids on such a bad road day. But no, nothing stopped lessons, neither rain, nor sleet, nor icy roads. Jean was picked to begin driving from the high school. The car full of teens was oddly silent as the Driver's Ed car slipped and slid through the first intersection. Jean struggled with the wheel, trying to correct the sure slide of the car toward the ditch just beyond the end of the school road. After her early trauma of the fish on her line, Jean learned to be *cool, man*! As an adolescent, she was never one to panic. No matter the situation, she held on tight and kept going. That is just what the Driver's Ed car did. It kept on going, going, going, out into the middle of the snowy field until the crust on top gave way and the tires sank into the farmland below. No one said a word as Jean put the shift level into Park and shut off the key. She turned to her teacher.

"Are you going to go for help, Mr. Smith, or do you want me to?"

Good for you Jeannie!

Cherish Every Moment.

CHAPTER 25

❧❦❧

Tree House Mishaps

As our younger boys grew into their mid-teens, and Jim passed his tenth birthday, all four of them campaigned for a tree house.

"We have lots of trees, Mom. Why not? It would be fun to build. We all can help."

The tallest pine tree with the thickest branches grew out near the end of the driveway. On a Saturday at the beginning of summer (no work driving bus then, vacation time!), I made a trip to a local lumber yard and brought home some 2x4s and a half dozen short planks for the flooring. True to their word, the guys turned out with hammers and a lot of enthusiasm, at least at first. When they discovered how tiring it is to pound nails, most of them faded away to ride bikes while Dad and I put together the simple platform of a tree house. Tom stuck around, climbing the outside branches of the tree, hanging on by his toenails it seemed, swinging the hammer like Tarzan building a wooden nest. At one point, the branch Tom stood on, broke beneath him and he tumbled to the ground.

"Tom, are you all right?" I asked from my perch high on a ladder.

"Sure, I'm OK," said Mister Macho Man as he dusted off his jeans.

I noticed he rubbed his bottom several times as he hunted among the fallen branches for his hammer. But I knew he would rather *die of a broken butt* than suffer the embarrassment of showing his mother the bruises. Teen boys! No matter how often I reminded them, they refused to acknowledge that I changed their diapers for eighteen months. To avoid any more accidents, I relinquished the ladder and offered it to Tom. He and Dad finished the tree house that afternoon.

Funny, once the structure was built, the boys spent very little time up there. Jim loved it, of course, being the youngest. He even went out early to wait for the bus that autumn, just so he could climb the tree and see the bus coming before the other kids. But his older siblings gradually shunned the tree house because they believed, at their mature ages of fourteen, sixteen, and seventeen, that it was not cool to climb trees anymore.

When these older, cooler, boys became interested in deer hunting, they began to realize the true value of a tree house. Hunters call them *tree stands*. Jay, Tom and Mike built a tree stand across the road in the woods owned by a sympathetic neighbor. Of course, they never caught sight of a deer in those woods. Too many noisy children in the area, and, legally, it was considered too close to the busy road where we lived. Eventually, the tree stand also suffered abandonment. So when we needed more lumber to finish building the car port for our expanding automobile collection (my car, Dave's truck and Rose's car), we tapped into the tree house for extra 2x4s.

It was another busy Saturday that spring. I always made bread on Saturdays but I took the time to go across the road to help Dave dismantle the boys' tree stand. I held the step ladder as he climbed up into the tree stand. He stepped out on a board and swung his hammer. Moments later, the ladder lay on its side and Dave was tumbling through the air, his body aimed at the ground below! Somehow during his fall, his flailing arms knocked the eyeglasses off his face. They flew through the air and landed under him. He still held the hammer in his hand as he stared up at me, a shocked expression on his face. He did look strange with his face stripped of glasses, his naked eyes wide and exposed, pupils huge with shock.

"Are you all right, Dave?" I asked, choking back a laugh. Truly, I did not know whether to howl with laughter or call the ambulance.

The shocked expression gave way to disgust as he flexed his muscles, testing for broken bones or unwanted piercing. He climbed to his feet, checking for blood or other damage. Nothing but injured pride. *Thank you, God!*

"That's enough of this horse manure!" he said, flinging his hammer into the weeds.

With a grunt and a groan, he gathered up his unbroken glasses and shoved them on his face.

By the time we gathered up the ladder, his hammer, and the board he had knocked out from beneath his feet, we were both giggling.

Cherish Every Moment.

CHAPTER 26

❦

All the Way to D.C. with Singing Sis

We are crowded into Joy and Ed's station wagon on our way to Washington, D.C. Mother, Dave and I share the back seat. My sister, Joy, and her husband, Ed, are up front. The radio is tuned to a Country/Western station. The beginning of a new song fills the heavy silence of the crowded car. Shelly West and David Frizzel harmonize, their voices full and mellow, as they sing, *"I'm sure missing you."*

I blink back tears. The words to the song zero in on my grief. Outside the car window, the full moon wanes as ribbons of pink and purple light up the dawn.

"Looks like it's going to be a fine day for traveling," Ed says. Joy nods agreement.

Beside me, our mother is silent, lost in her own heavy thoughts. Her brow is furrowed, her lips move in silent prayer. She counts off the beads of a red plastic rosary with her gnarled old fingers. The date is April 1, 1981 and we are on our way south to my baby brother's funeral. I wonder if Mother remembers that today is also the thirteenth anniversary of her husband's death.

Of course she remembers, I chide myself. My heart aches with pity for her two great losses, her husband, then her beloved son. Jim was in his mid-thirties when he had a bad reaction to prescription drugs. His wife found him sprawled across their bed when she returned from her job as night nurse at a Washington, D.C. hospital. My brother could not be revived.

As the car speeds south toward our nation's Capital, the sun comes up, warming the interior of the car, if not my inner thoughts. I feel cold, numb with shock and grief. I am restless, squirming, trying to wiggle away from the vast emptiness of my mourning soul.

Oh God, oh God, oh God, where are you?

How could my baby brother, Jimbo the clown boy, be dead?

He was born just after New Year's in 1945, a miracle baby, birthed by my middle-aged mother, her last chance to produce a son. My sisters were sixteen and fourteen when Jimbo was born. I was almost nine. As Jimbo grew up, we became very close. He loved our kids and was our first babysitter. Often, he drove out to our Eden home for a weekend, just to spend time with his big Sis and all those kids. Our children loved him, crowding around him, leaping into his arms, as soon as he appeared in the kitchen doorway. We shared a silly irreverent humor that made us laugh hysterically at nothing in particular.

One summer, when our family was visiting Mother in Kenmore, Jimbo, sixteen, our cousin Leo, then around twenty, and I went for a bicycle ride.

There had been a report of a tornado touch-down near the high school. We pedaled down the middle of the streets of Kenmore, each trying to outdo the other in speed and endurance. Frankly, I felt winded and out of breath by the time we coasted into the parking lot of the school. *Too many babies, not enough exercise,* I thought, stepping down near a group of young teens.

Brother Jimbo

The tallest of the group, a cool cat with slicked back hair, *The Elvis Look*, gave us a mocking smile.

"What? Is this, Old Fogies on Bicycles Week?" he sneered.

Leo, highly insulted, dropped his bike and went after the smart aleck. Jimbo and I cracked up laughing. The group of teens scattered before Leo's wrath. Jimbo and I pedaled our sore leg muscles back toward our mother's house, laughing our way home. Leo grumbled behind us. "I didn't think it was so funny." We laughed even harder.

My Jimbo, gone? Not possible.

Brother Jim, who taught himself to play guitar at age thirty and recorded songs on cassettes to serenade our delighted Mother, our Jimbo, gone? *Can't be!*

In the car on that long journey south, the song comes on the radio again. Incredibly, I start to sing along.

"I'm sure missing you. I'm sure missing you."

I cannot believe he is dead. In fact, I entertain magical thinking, a way of denying the too-painful truth. It is a trick, something to do with his job at the Pentagon. Jimbo can't be dead!

On that long ride south, squeezed in the back seat between Dave and Mother, that song keeps reminding me of our loss.

"I'm sure missing you. I'm sure missing you."

Have you ever thought about song, what a gift it is? Just when, in the long annuals of time, did people begin to mimic the birds of the air and the howl of wolves? In church, in our cars, in the privacy of our homes, even in supermarkets (guilty!), we open our throats and lift our voices in song. In the Old Testament, David, son of Jesse, the lowly shepherd boy who later became the King of Israel, often endeared himself to King Saul by singing. Saul, who suffered from serious depression, would be soothed by David's psalms played on the lyre, a stringed musical instrument. Song, a gift from God to lift our hearts when we are sad, a reminder of special events long since past.

That day in the car on the way to Washington, the song plays over and over, at least once every hour. Every time it comes on the radio, I join in.

"I'm sure missing you."

My sister Joy, the no-nonsense sister whose reaction to our brother's death is revealed in anger, turns around to chide me for singing.

"All the way to Washington D.C. with singing Sis," she says with a scowl.

Beside me, Mother glances my way. Her gnarled old fingers tap my knee.

"Go ahead and sing, Ceil. I like hearing it."

Joy heaves a long sigh and turns around. Mother gives me the first smile I have seen since we broke the terrible news to her last evening. She nods in encouragement and gestures toward the radio.

"Sing, girl."

Obediently, I sing. But even without Mother's encouragement, I would have continued to sing. Songs echo in my head all the time. Every situation I encounter during my long busy days, reminds me of some song I have heard in the past.

Walk the dog? *"Walking My Baby Back Home."*
Snowing outside? *"Winter Wonderland."*

Taking a grandson for a walk, hand in hand? We sing, the *Do-Wah Diddy*, song.

Songs light up my interior darkness when sadness captures me. In fact, if I get to the Golden Gates, I hope to tell St. Peter, *"I'm here for the singing."*

Later that evening, our family gathered together, including Betty and Len, who flew down from Detroit, and cousin Leo, who drove down to be with us. As we huddle together in the funeral parlor, the truth finally sinks in. I am still in denial, pretending we are just disinterested visitors gathered to attend a stranger's Wake. I glance up. Above the door to my brother's bier, his name juts out into the hallway. Gold letters on a shiny black background spell the end to my hopes and magical dreams.

James C. Ramier.

It's true, my brother is dead.

Too painful to think about. We cling together, we endure.

My younger brother has been gone for twenty-eight years. Yet, if a Country/Western singer on RFD-TV, begins that favorite old song, I join in, swallowing the lump in my throat and singing every word through long-remembered grief.

"I'm sure missing you. I'm sure missing you."

Cherish Every Moment.

❦

CHAPTER 27

Wearry's Mad

Our youngest daughter, Rose, gave birth to a handsome little boy that June of 1981. Blond and blue-eyed like his parents, I held this precious bundle while he was still warm from the womb.

Mother and baby were living in our upstairs apartment at that time since Rose and her hubby were having relationship difficulties. By the time the adults reconciled, Larry was walking and beginning to talk. A sunny, happy little boy, his grin always made my heart turn over with pride and love. But something happened during those early formative years. Maybe too many vocal arguments? The word, "*Shut up!*" shouted too often between his parents? In any event, while Rose carried the unborn sister who would become Anna, Larry suddenly lost his way with words. He refused to speak at all. No *Mommy*, no *Daddy*, not even the most popular word of every two year old toddler, "*No!*" escaped Larry's lips.

We asked him, "Why won't you talk, Larry?"

Larry wouldn't say.

But he did have a way of communicating. He screamed. And he threw spectacular tantrums. Inside the angry boy the sunny toddler still lurked, but no one seemed skilled enough to break through his raging muteness.

One fine summer's day, while visiting us, four-year-old Larry discovered our backyard garden. He loved the tall sweet-corn plants. Dressed in shorts and a green tee shirt (his favorite color), he ran through the corn stalks, arms out, corn stalk leaves brushing his face. How he smiled and chuckled as he ran through the corn! Even his mother, holding daughter Anna on one hip while trying to corral the excited toddler, had to pause and smile fondly as Larry grinned from ear to ear. Rose had her hands full every day, caring for the baby, plus dealing with the stress of her son's frequent, violent (and puzzling to all of us) tantrums, Running through the corn, this troubled child of God seemed perfectly normal, and *happy* for a change. An unforgettable memory for me, carved on my heart.

But these sweet times were few and scattered. Most of the time Larry screamed like a wild thing at anything and everything. His parents were at their wits' end. Fear marked Rose's face every time she struggled and failed to calm Larry down from one of his fierce rages.

"What's wrong with him, Mom?" she asked me, tears of frustration filling her eyes.

I had no easy answers for my daughter's dilemma. With a houseful of children, we had dealt with our share of angry toddlers down through the years, but nothing like this. The terrible labels *retarded* or *autistic* were too frightening to even mention.

"Maybe Larry should be evaluated?" I hesitated to suggest it. But something needed to be done for the boy. He was almost four years old and still not communicating with words. "Ask your Pediatrician about it, Rose."

Finally, after many delays and some serious paperwork, Larry had an appointment at the Speech and Hearing Clinic at Children's

Hospital in Buffalo. I went along for moral support and to care for the toddler Anna while her wild-thing brother and Rose went into a therapy room for his evaluation.

Anna and I sat on plastic chairs in a children's waiting room. Toys, most of them missing parts, or rather dirty, littered the floor. Anna had her own *lovey* to cling to, a clown doll. She sat in my lap, contented to watch the other children in the room as they played. Rose and Larry disappeared into a long hallway. We sat and waited. Time seemed to slow down.

I stared out the window at a dreary Buffalo winter day, all grays and black, dark leafless trees and dirty snow. The old building creaked like a crumbling castle in a heavy wind. I shuddered, swept away by fear of the future. *What happened to our happy little boy, the smiling child in the corn? What will the Powers That Be decide about Larry's future?*

Suddenly, from deep in the old building, a strange and frightening sound began. *Thump! Bump! Thump!* The heavy sounds echoed down the hallway. Windows seemed to vibrate with the force of something too big to be contained within the flimsy walls of the waiting room.

"What is that?" A mother asked. Her little boy climbed into her lap and popped his thumb into his mouth.

"A monster!" one child shrilled.

Other children leapt at their parents and whimpered in fear.

Thump! Bump! Thump! Rattle! More thumps. The noise grew louder. Screams were added to the thumps and bumps. The adults in the room stared at each other, fear reflected on each puzzled face.

In my lap, Anna hugged her clown. She leaned against me and sighed.

"Wearry's mad," she said and popped her thumb into her mouth.

Larry and Anna

At almost three years old, Anna had a little problem with her L sounds.

"Oh! *Larry's* mad?" I whispered.

She nodded and hugged her clown. I stared around at the other parents. No way would I tell them that the monster down the hall was just our four-year-old having a tantrum. Let them be afraid. Their fear matched my own. What would happen to my grandson now?

A few moments later, Rose came to the door. She had tears on her cheeks. She reached for Anna.

"Mom, they want to see you, too."

The three of us hustled down the hallway to a metal door. The thumping and bumping stopped as we stepped through the doorway. Larry lay on the floor, kicking at the door. He rolled away when he saw me, then his screams turned to pitiful sobs. He lifted his arms and I picked him up. Despite the cool room, he was drenched with sweat from the exertion of his violent tantrum. I smoothed his hair and he quieted immediately. We sat down on the third chair next to the therapist. She smiled and made a note in his file.

"I just wanted to see the whole family dynamics," she said.

Immediately, I felt guilty. Had I contributed to Larry's situation? Was it *me* making him so angry? When I asked, she shook her head.

"Now Grandma, don't fret. We can help this young man."

Beside me, Rose heaved a long sigh and bit back tears of relief.

The people at the Speech and Hearing Clinic were true to their word. Within a month of beginning therapy Larry was speaking in sentences. Of course, many of the words were angry words, but he was talking. At last!

Cherish Every Moment

But Larry's story does not end there. Because of his delayed speech, he was put into a Special Needs program. He attended remedial classes in school for most of his elementary years, but by high school, Larry's sharp intellect broke through. The boy is a whiz with numbers.

He graduated with honors from high school, went on to college. Last year, he graduated *Cum Laude* with a degree in Accounting.

While in his last year of high school, he learned to drive. His first long solo trip had him driving down to visit us, a journey of over one hundred miles. Saint Christopher heard a lot of fervent prayers that day, believe me. When his little red car finally pulled around our house, I leaped up with joyful relief. Standing in the kitchen, looking down through the sliding glass door at our grandson sitting in the driver's seat, my heart slid back in time.

I saw a little boy running through the corn. Grinning from ear to ear. Now the somehow grown up Larry was grinning up at me from the front seat of his very own car.

Larry, in his mid-twenties now, has his own apartment and is saving to buy a house. He comes down quite often to visit. He is a great help to both Grandpa and me with the tougher work of running a country property. His boisterous laughter echoes through the house as he beats us at cards, again! Who would think that angry little boy would turn out to be such a blessing to the whole family? *Thank you, God, for Larry.*

Cherish Every Moment

CHAPTER 28

❧❦❧

The Fye Fazzer and Other Weird Family Labels

Isn't it strange and truly wonderful how human language evolves? From the first grunted efforts, accompanied by the pointing of a chubby finger, children learn to speak the language native to their families. "Uhhh!" and a finger jabbed toward a favored toy, brings happy results. The mom or dad smile, speak in high pitched, delighted tones, and give the toy its name.

"Ball? Baby wants ball?"

The baby smiles and points again. "Buhhhh!"

Which brings more smiles from the delirious parent, and words that reinforce the speech lesson.

"Ball? Baby wants *ball!*"

Strikingly familiar in voice tone and excitement to the way we train puppies.

""Go out? Puppy wants to go out? Good doggie!"

It is a wonder the child does not also pant and wag his tail, like a puppy does when faced with the same scenario.

In any event, most children do learn to speak, making their needs known by one way or another. Sometimes it takes a bit of trail and error before the speech rookie hits the right combination of vowels and consonants.

For example, our oldest son, Davy, by very virtue of his being the first-born, had to wing it, more or less. No older siblings to teach him proper language skills, or make fun of his mistakes, which is sometimes the best way to learn something as difficult as speaking English. He learned the basics from listening to me talk or sing to the babies. Of course, this was before Elvis, the Rolling Stones, and Mick Jagger introduced us into Rock and Roll music whose lyrics delighted in using ungrammatical language. *"Can't get no, sat-is-faction!"*

I have a weird memory for old song lyrics and often sang the babies to sleep with Golden Oldies such as, *"Walking My Baby Back Home,"* or *"Hush Little Baby,"* or any of the other songs I learned growing up in the 1940's.

In any event, Davy came up with some really interesting labels for common objects. Both he and his younger brother Russ wore suspenders to keep their pants up. Being hipless wonders from the time the bulky diapers came off, the boys needed help to remain modestly dressed. Davy called them, "Benders." The name stuck. Even today, when Grandpa Dave is forced to wear both belt and suspenders to keep his pants up, we still call them benders.

Cathy, at age two, while recovering from a tonsillectomy, croaked, "Bink of wa-wa, Mommy?"

Even today, a senior citizen trying to stay fit, when I return from a vigorous walk, I reach for a bottle of cold water, and tell myself, "Need a bink of wa-wa, Mommy?"

By far, the favorite mispronunciation is "Fye Fazzer" Need a handy tool to swat a pesky bug? Reach for the fye fazzer. The entire Bauer family now uses the term. Sort of a secret family code word, it is accompanied by a rolling of the eyes and a sentimental grin as we swat away the pesky bugs of summer with the nearest fye fazzer.

Last summer, I had the privilege of helping out our nephew, Butch, as he rested at home in the Hospice Program. My job was to sit with him between the time his wife left for work and his mother-in-law arrived, too few meaningful hours spent with my favorite nephew.

Butch had been our guardian angel when we built our house in the woods. He stopped every day after his job and checked out the progress we had made that day. Following his sage advice, we had constructed the walls flat on the floor, plywood nailed to the 2x6's shell frame.

"Ah, I see you have two walls built. Be right back," he said.

Minutes later, Butch would return with a driveway full of friends and they would raise the walls for us. Now, years later, I felt privileged to be asked to sit with him as he waited for God to take him home to heaven. An angel waiting to fly.

We talked about many things, laughed at funny videos or movies, and sometimes, just sat there at peace, glad to have those few hours together. But the first day I arrived at his enclosed front porch, a red wasp followed me in the door. I tried to urge it back out the door with my purse. No deal! It was determined to fly around looking for trouble. I am allergic to its sting, so I wasted little time trying to save its miserable life.

"Butch!" I yelled into the front window, which overlooked his hospice bed. "Where's your fye fazzer?"

Butch had been dozing. His eyes flew open.

"What? What are you talking about? Fye fazzer!" and he laughed as he remembered.

"The *fly swatter* is hanging up next to the door."

He shook his head and grinned.
"Look out, bug! Crazy lady with a weapon!"
But he laughed about it all afternoon.
Thanks Ravy-Davy for your colorful language.
           Cherish Every Moment.

CHAPTER 29

❦

Cucumbers and Cards

If you marry into a German family, you better believe that eating cucumbers and playing cards will always be a vital part of your life.

In our neck to the woods, cucumber vines snake through every housewife's garden and creamed cucumbers and onions grace every summer-time table. Although my mother was 100% Irish, she too lived in the Pennsylvania countryside as a girl. Garden fresh produce remained an important part of her diet, as well as our family's as we grew up. Dave's mother, a farm wife who remained a gifted cook all her life, shared with me her delicious recipe for creamed cucumbers.

Family traditions, plus the constant demand for fresh produce to supplement our diet, meant we too had a big garden every summer. Creamed cucumbers graced our table then as now, a popular dish, easy to make and always well appreciated. How well appreciated? You'll see!

When son Dave married, he was working at the Ford plant and lived not far from our house in Eden. He and his wife, Sue, had two boys, Dave III and Chris, eighteen months apart in age.

We frequently invited them over on Sundays, for supper and to play cards in the evening. One summer's day, the grandsons had been playing hard outside. Dave III was four, his younger brother Chris, barely three. When I announced supper, they came rushing into the kitchen, with big smiles and dusty hands. Little Davy jumped up on the long bench to survey the food.

"Oh boy! Cucumbers!" he said.

His mother already had Chris by the hand to escort him into the bathroom for a wash job.

"Now, Davy!" she warned. "Don't you *dare* touch those cucumbers with those dirty hands."

Davy grinned. Holding his hands behind his back, he leaned over the cucumber dish and fished out a slice with his teeth!

"Yum!" he said, crunching away as his Mom dragged him off the bench.

Another family legend, unforgettable.

That evening, after the dishes were done, we dug out the Euchre deck to play cards. This popular game is played with four people, who form partners—us against them. We use the seven highest cards, ace through nine, of each suit. It is a fast game with a small deck of twenty-four cards. Half a pinochle deck works well and gives us an extra deck for future use. Five cards are dealt to each person, with four remaining for the "head deck." The top card on the head deck is turned over and may become trump. Each player is given a chance to either accept or decline the trump card. The game is played quickly with much table pounding and laughter when one or the other set of partners are either successful, or not.

"Euchre!" A shout of triumph as someone fails to make their required tricks.

The deal comes around quickly, passed clockwise around the table as each set of partners strives to outdo the others in tricks taken. The game ends when one side scores ten points.

As we played cards that evening, young Dave III sat on his mother's lap, scanning her cards, frowning as he struggled to learn the strategy of the game. When the deck passed to his mother, Davy made a grab for them.

"My turn to shubble," he said. He meant *shuffle* the cards, but members of our entire family now uses his mispronunciation when it is their turn to deal.

"My turn to shubble."

All the children in our extended families learned how to play cards at an early age. I was only eight when my parents allowed me to sit in on their weekly poker game. They called it *penny ante* since they played for money. Most games began with an ante of a nickel. Raises came in two-cent increments and were limited to three raises per hand. Never a money-raising scheme, those long ago games were played for mere pocket change, and the chance to socialize with friends and relatives. At the end of the evening, the pennies were scooped up into old jelly jars, and put away until next time. The host of the evening usually put on a little spread, a light lunch. My mother specialized in home-baked beans and freshly baked white bread. Occasionally, if her two apple trees had a good year, she baked pies. My birth family never lacked for company to socialize.

No television in those days of my childhood, just a floor modal Zenith radio, which gave families the news of the day, and not much else. People got together to play cards, or Dominoes, or Chinese checkers. As children of 1940's, my sisters and I kept busy playing games also. Children of that era were expected to entertain themselves. We played Old Maid, Authors, Go Fish, and my favorite, Rummy. This is how we had fun with our friends. We often played wild games of hide & seek, or kick the can, outside in the spooky darkness. Our parents did not worry about our safety as we played outside after dark. Neighbors knew each other then, everyone kept an eye out for the youngsters. Sometimes, we played our games in the street. Traffic remained light, few people could afford a car. People who had cars did not drive fast, just in case an excited child might dart out in front of them. Life was good and we enjoyed every moment.

Fast forward sixty years. We are still playing Euchre every chance we get. Every family gathering, every time another couple comes over for a visit, the cards come out. We have been playing the game so long, it is unfair for me to be Dave's partner because I know his strategy so well. A hesitation as he scans his hand of cards, translates to: *I have some trump but not enough to make it without my partner's help*. I play an aggressive, risk-taking game. It bothers me not a whit to be euchred. Dave is more conservative and a bit of a sand-bagger (holds enough trump to name the suit, but passes in the hope of euchring someone). So, if Dave hesitates over his cards, and we are partners, I will name trump in a heart-beat, and *laugh* if I guess wrong and lose to the other side. Makes the game interesting to take chances, don't you know?

Several of our children and grandchildren play the game using the style I taught them. Jason, Mike, and Larry are a few of these dare-devils. Somehow, they seem to be blessed with great good luck. Now if they would only learn not to *gloat* when they euchre Grandpa, things might calm down a little at our game table. There are two types of card players, the fun lovers, like me and the other dare-devils, and the *serious* players (like Dave) who get pretty upset when the cards seem stacked against them. Grandpa Dave becomes so incensed by the raucous mocking laughter of the lucky winners, he may up and refuse to play cards at all. His loss. In a family as large as ours, there are always willing players to fill his vacated chair.

At a family gathering recently, Dave III, now a father of three children, sat with his youngest on his lap as we played

Euchre. Maya was barely a year old, but she studied her dad's cards with the same concentration he exhibited as a toddler thirty years ago.

"My turn to shubble."

Cherish Every Moment.

* * *

We can't finish this chapter about playing cards without mentioning Pinochle.

While living in California, our daughter-in-law, Andrea (Jim's wife), used to come over every morning before her work shift to eat breakfast with us. She had been raised in the same pocket of devoted card players as our family and loved to play any card game. She and Jim used to play Euchre during lunch period at school, a common occurrence in the Eden school. The cool students refused to eat at lunch time, they played cards instead. Many of these young adults came from poor families who couldn't afford to buy lunch. It was not cool to bring a brown bag from home, either. So card games flourished. Euchre is a game best played with four players. We only had three people in our kitchen those sunny mornings in California: Dave, Andrea and me. We usually played Rummy or Uno.

One day Andrea discovered that Dave and I used to play Pinochle. In fact we had belonged to a Pinochle club and played every week at my parents' home. At that time, early in our marriage, we had two tables of players, my sisters and their husbands, Mother and Pop, plus Dave and me.

Then as now, Dave was a cautious player. One game, when Betty's husband, Len, was his partner, Dave held double Pinochle in his hand (both queens of spades and both jacks of diamonds). This lucky combination is worth thirty points in meld. Len had a medium to good hand, but not enough to outbid the opposing team. When it came time to meld out (lay the meld cards on the table to be counted for points), Dave laid down his double Pinochle. Len blew up. He too was a *serious* card player and he really lit into Dave about not supporting his bid.

Dave, embarrassed and insulted, stood up and left the house. I found him sitting in our car, waiting to go home. That ended our Pinochle career, no more card club for us.

Andrea, excited about playing a more interesting game like Pinochle, instead of the eternal Uno and mind-numbing Rummy, urged us to play the game. Dave refused.

"Oh no! I'm not about to get yelled at again because I didn't speak up about my meld. No, no way."

Andrea, not one to become easily discouraged, dragged out our family *Bible*. Both she and I laid a hand on the Bible and swore not to scold Dave if he made a mistake while playing cards. Finally, he agreed to learn the game all over again. We spent many delightful mornings playing three-handed Pinochle, or *cutthroat* as it is called. This is another game we taught our grandchildren, and another card game with which they excel.

"Remember, Larry, no gloating!"

Cherish Every Moment.

CHAPTER 30

That
Fearsome "F" Word

What is there about the most dreaded of F words—*forty, forty, forty*—that drives women crazy? Is it the passage of too much time, the fear of a dismal future complete with wrinkles, gray hair, and sagging butts? Whatever the reasoning, turning the big 4-O triggers a sea change in every woman's life. Some women face their forties by opting for a face lift, lipo-suction, going blonde, or taking on a new, younger lover.

By the time I hit forty, we already had four grandsons, and our youngest son, Jim, just turned eight. I was working two jobs, and struggling to deal with the sea change in our family as the older pollywogs left the pond. Davy and Cathy both had children of their own, Russ had disappeared into the wilds of southern California, and Barb lived in Pennsylvania with her soon to be husband, Tom. Jean left right after her high school graduation. The half of our family still at home, Rose, Jason, Thomas, Mike and Jim, rattled around in our seven-bedroom house. My hair, which had begun to show gray at a very early age, now considered Miss Clairol a personal friend. Wrinkles did not bother me until I turned fifty. My aging body kept in pretty good shape thanks to driving a school bus with a standard shift. The clutch work toned my legs. The reach and pull of the long handled passenger door kept my arms firm. My lifetime lover still slept beside me every night. Mid-life crisis? Who had time?

I was in my mid-forties before I had time to realize that I should be acting out, having a meltdown about growing older. Actually, the melting was easy enough. Every night I melted into the sheets as waves of hot flashes drenched my night clothes. I cried a lot, missing my grown up girls, and Dave claimed I was crabby, too. *Such loyalty!* I thought, fanning myself with a magazine. *Plain to see he doesn't have nightly meltdowns.* So what radical thing could I do to slide through my forties with ease and grace?

I hit the roads on a motorcycle.

Hey, what's not to love about zooming down a country road on two wheels, wind whipping hair out the back of my helmet, cool breezes blowing away my sweaty migraine headache, bees down my shirt? In my blue imitation-leather jacket, jeans tucked into high top sneakers, and star-spangled helmet with a red heart on the back of it, I felt *cool, man!* A bonus was the embarrassment I inflicted on my two youngest sons, Mike and Jim, whose friends gave them the business about their, "Motorcycle Mama."

It actually began as an economy move. This happened during the gas shortage of the late 1970's. I worked for the local school, driving a big yellow bus. Twice a day, I drove the four miles down to the bus garage, and back again. A Moped made sense, gas-wise. In fact, other drivers also jumped on the cycle bandwagon. We had an unofficial club, the Yellow Angels. Six drivers rode Mopeds, the mechanics rode full sized motorcycles. I wrote an article about it for the local paper, and we all had our picture in *The Buffalo Evening News.* But our loyal affair with the small cycles soon waned.

One driver said, "I hate it when I get swept off the road by the oil truck."

I agreed. Maybe it was the notoriety of the Yellow Angels making us local targets, but we all seemed to share the feeling of being little riders in a too big world. I was the first bus driver to trade up to a full sized Honda 200 cc. After riding the tiny Moped, this full sized cycle seemed like a lot of machine to me.

Son Jason, who had joined the Air Force right out of high school, was home from England where he had been stationed. He went along with us to Cycle World as we brought home my new wheels in the back of Dave's truck. He helped muscle the cycle down from the truck bed and stood back, gesturing for me to get on and ride.

"It's raining," I said. This was a thin excuse, because, to tell the truth, I was a bit hesitant to get on and ride the big beast.

Dave stepped up. "I'll take it around the house to check it out for you, Honey."

Sounded good to me.

Dave heaved one leg over the cycle and pulled on the clutch lever on the left side of the handlebar. The right side handle-grip held the accelerator. His left foot found the shift pedal.

"Remember Dave, the shift pattern is one down and three up," I told him, repeating the sales person's instructions.

Carefully, he let out the clutch and the cycle lurched out of the garage. We all watched, as he managed to shift into second gear while passing our bedroom window. He hit third as he passed the swing set on the opposite side of the house. For a minute or so he was out of sight as he zoomed around the front of the house.

"Sounds like Dad is in fourth gear," Jason said, taking a long sip from his cup of coffee.

The cycle roared down the driveway, headed for the garage. It was coming fast, too fast. At the entrance to the garage, the front tire hit a large piece of gravel and began to tilt and slide. As the cycle and its rider slid past Jason, he sucked in his body and crowded against the garage wall beside the garbage cans. His coffee slopped over his hand. Fear flickered briefly in his eyes as the cycle slid past the garbage containers and left narrow tire tracks on the side of the metal cans. Jason checked his shoes for skid marks.

"Whoa! Whoa!" Dave roared, reverting to his farm boy training when dealing with a balky team of horses.

The cycle, with Dave still on board, slid sidewards under the lawn tractor. The back tire still spun wildly as I reached across the handlebars and hit the kill switch. Blessed silence in the garage, except for the sound of Jason choking on his coffee.

Dave on motorcycle

"Are you all right, Dear?" I said, trying not to laugh out loud.

Dave struggled to climb out from under the cycle. He accepted my hand with a scowl of embarrassment on his face.

"I couldn't find the clutch or the brake," he said, waving his left foot. "The tighter I held on, the faster we went!"

"That's because the accelerator was in your right hand, Dear," I said, in a strangled voice.

He glared at the damaged cycle. "Broke the back turn-signal, darn it!" he said.

Behind us Jason lost his well-fought attempt at control. He burst into wild laughter. I joined him. Dave flushed a bright red and spoke the words that virtually ended his career as a rider of two-wheeled vehicles.

"That's enough of this horse manure!" he said.

Cherish Every Moment.

❧

CHAPTER 31

The Eyeball Cup and
Other Family Favorites

While living in California, one of our daughters, Jean, gave birth to a baby boy. She lived out in the "boonies" as she called them, the barely-reclaimed- from-the-desert country north of Sacramento. Her son, JR grew up isolated from other children, and consequently very shy. One day Jean brought her little boy, then a two-year-old toddler, to visit. She needed dental work and so left the boy with me for two hours.

As soon as the door closed on his mother's familiar form, JR began to cry. He cried and cried. Nothing I said or did comforted him. He wanted Mommy. No one else would do. Finally, frustrated at my lack of grandmotherly skills with this crying child, I put him into our bedroom for time out. He howled louder.

"Now, JR," I said calmly (at least I tried to be calm!). "When you stop crying you can come out of the bedroom. I'm going to watch Barney," I said, trying to coax him out of his misery. No use. I sat down on the recliner watch the children's program, trying to ignore the wailing behind me. Occasionally, I swivelled around to glance down the long hallway to the bedroom. The

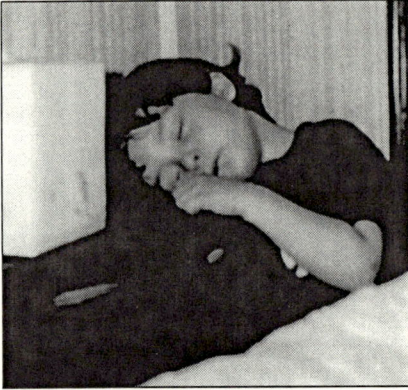

JR falls asleep standing up

toddler usually stood in the doorway. As soon as he saw me turn, JR would duck back inside the room and howl louder. After a bit, despite the noise behind me, I got interested in Barney's song and dance routines. A while longer, when the program changed to a Rural Report, I noticed something strange and almost frightening. *Silence. Silence in the house!*

I swivelled around quickly. No little boy standing and sniffling in the hallway. No JR ducking back into the bedroom. Did he fall asleep? I leaped up and walked quickly down to the bedroom. My first glance into the bedroom revealed an empty bed. My heard did a little flip-flop.

Where is he? I didn't heard the back door open, but maybe...

Stepping into the bedroom I struggled to smother a giggle of relief. Standing in the corner, behind the blue hamper, his head resting on top of the hamper, JR snored gently, sound asleep in his upright position. I ran to grab the camera. Now, at age twenty, JR is a tall, handsome guy with a steady girlfriend. When they came East to visit last summer, I took special delight in showing her the picture of JR, standing behind the hamper, sound asleep.

"Now here is a guy who can sleep standing up!"

But it is to JR, the toddler, that we owe the label, The Eyeball Cup.

That same visit, after his mother returned from the dentist, we had lunch together. I brought out our assortment of plastic cups and gave him a choice.

"Which cup would you like to use, JR?"

He whispered something into Jean's ear. She laughed and pointed at a red cup, a Kool- Aid promotional cup, with a smiling face and googly-eyes.

"He wants the Eyeball Cup."

Fast forward twenty years. We still have the cup. Now it is our great-grandchildren who fight over The Eyeball Cup.

The grandchildren and great-grandchildren also fight over other oddball possessions. For instance, we have two golden forks and one golden spoon. Somehow the rumor got started (I think Grandpa passed the word), "*Only good kids get a golden fork or the golden spoon.*"

Funny how something out of the ordinary influences family traditions. The great-grandkids fight over who deserves to use the golden tableware.

"I was good today, Grandma, right?" Devin insists.

Alex chimes in, "I'm *always* good, right Grandma?"

"OK boys, you both get a golden fork tonight."

Devin is eight now, old enough to think things through. Last visit he asked, "Grandma? Where did you get the golden forks?"

I rolled my eyes at his parents, our oldest grandson, Dave III and his wonderful wife, Tina. They both grinned, knowing some outrageous tale might come out right about now. I do have a reputation as a story teller to uphold, you know!

"Well Devin, sometimes Grandpa and I go shopping at a very special store. They have wonderful old things there, and the prices are always nice and low so we can afford them."

Devin knew about affording stuff. His parents kept a pretty tight budget, as most young families do these days.

"What's the name of that special store, Grandma?"

"It is a marvelous store, called The Goodwill Store."

He turned excitedly toward his parents. "Can we go there sometime, Mom?"

Tina, bless her, hid her grin and nodded solemnly. The boys still fight over the golden forks.

Another family favorite worthy of a family squabble is the high stool. The stool, a bar stool with a back, is actually mine. We bought it to save my weak back whenever I have serious baking to do. I have learned to roll out pie crust while sitting on the stool. It also gets lots of use when it is apple-peeling time in the fall. We have friends who give us apples from their trees. Dave helps as we make lots of applesauce for the winter.

The family rule is, the youngest person at the table gets to sit in the high stool. Sometimes it is a grandchild, other times a great-grandchild. Sometimes, when it is an adult only meal time, the youngest person might be Dave's youngest brother John. Sometimes, I am the youngest. The rule holds true, even though our adult grandson Larry wants to claim the high stool on occasion. Whoever is the youngest, gets the honor of being tall diner.

The first time Alex, a great-grandson, sat in the high stool, he wiggled with excitement. We had mini-turkey subs that day for lunch. These are made with hot dog rolls, sliced turkey lunch meat, cheese, lettuce and mayonnaise. Alex took a big bite and ended up with mayo on his chin.

"Alex, wipe your face," Tina said. She meant, of course, "*Use your napkin!*"

The toddler, sitting on the high stool with our everyday tablecloth hanging into his lap, did the expected thing (at least it seemed reasonable to me!). He picked up the edge of the tablecloth and swiped at his mouth.

Grandpa and I jumped up to leave the room. We didn't want to usurp the authority of Alex's parents by howling with laughter.

Cherish Every Moment.

❧❧❧

CHAPTER 32

Freeze-dried Diapers and Other Rituals of Antiquity

Dave and I had been married less than a year when my father took us to the furniture and appliance store where he worked part-time in the evenings and weekends. Pop also had a full time job at Dunlap Tire and Rubber during the day, but he needed extra cash for Jimbo's college fund. At Omel's Fine Furniture, we picked out a top-of-the-line Blackstone wringer washer. The cost (even with my father's employee's discount) was beyond our limited budget, so we financed it. Pop co-signed the loan for $69, five dollars a month until it was paid off. It seems laughable now, the small cost for a major appliance back then. Today that same amount barely covers our retirement weekly food bill at Walmart! But that happened in the 1950's, the good old days, as we senior citizens are fond of saying in the light of today's ridiculous living costs.

I cannot count how many thousands of diapers churned in that big laundry tub, nor how many times I fed diapers through those oversized wringer rollers. Oh yes, diapers, *real cloth diapers* were used on our babies! It was a different world back then. Many remember it as a better world. Babies wore cloth diapers, which when soiled, were rinsed out in the commode, then soaked in a diaper pail under the sink until the pail was full. Often it was the sharp odor of ammonia from the soiled diapers that stung our noses and prompted the ritual of baby laundry. First the water from reeking diaper pail was emptied into the nearest commode. Down in the basement, the contents of the pail were dumped into the washer tub, hot water and a little bit of bleach added, then churned five minutes. Then we hit the lever that drained the dirty water into the laundry tub, then refilled the washer with hot water and more soap. Ivory Flakes was the recommended soap for diapers, but with our mineral-rich well water, I had to use something else to make enough suds. After twenty minutes (more if I got involved with baby bottles or baby burping, or baby bathing), the diapers were fished out of the hot soapy water and put through the wringer.

My mother-in-law once remarked, "You don't wash the dirty clothes, Cecile, you *scald* them clean!" She meant it as a compliment, I think.

We had to use a stick to fish out the diapers in order to feed them through the wringer. These hot slippery diapers dropped from the wringer into a tub of cold water, then wrung again into a second tub of water, then fed again into the wringer and into the waiting laundry basket below. The wringer assembly swivelled in a complete arc to accommodate the various positions needed to complete the laundry dance.

Then came the fun part: hanging the diapers outside on the clothesline. For some reason incomprehensible to any normal person, I loved doing laundry. Maybe it was the dirty-to-clean process that seemed so satisfying. Or perhaps it was the time alone down cellar that I cherished, away from the wild commotion of children playing, fighting, crying or needing something *right now,*

Mom! In any event, hanging the diapers outside always seemed a special event to me. I loved the faint scent of baby, the whiteness of innocence flapping on the line, the relative silence in my child-sensitive ears as only the sounds of birds singing, or trees rustling, or wind howling, soothed my soul. I hung diapers outside even during the cold winters of Western New York, and many-a-time they froze on the line. After a bit, the wind would flap them dry. My neighbor Betty, used to say, "Your laundry is freeze-dried." Betty owned a drier, but we never had one until I gave birth to my seventh child, Jason, and my parents invested in a pair of "laundry twins" for me.

News flash: I still hang my laundry outside, winter or summer. Must be addicted to the wonderful scent of line-dried sheets and towels.

Last summer, when our grandson's family visited, I did some laundry one morning. As I carried out the full basket of sheets and towels, great-grandson Devin watched me with astonished eyes.

"What are you doing, Grandma?"

Like an echo, his younger brother Alex said, "What are you doing, Grandma?"

"Guess!" I said, bending down to lift a wet sheet and pin it to the clothesline strung between two trees.

Like twins echoing their speech, they both said again, "What are you doing, Grandma?"

I know that game, too. "Guess!" I said.

Devin hazarded a wild guess. "*Laundry?*"

I had to laugh at the incredulousness in his voice. He had never witnessed such a strange event, someone hanging wet clothing or bedding on a clothesline outside. Made me nostalgic for the good old days, when each housewife tried to be the first woman with her clothesline filled on Monday morning.

When we lived in California in a mobile home park, the management frowned on the hanging of laundry outside. The written rules posted prominently in the clubhouse even prohibited hanging throw rugs over the railings of our porch. Such fuddy-duddys! Dave rigged up a metal pipe across two upright pieces that could not be seen from the street. I draped my laundry over plastic hangers and hung them on the line. No one tells *me* not to air dry my laundry! I still grin when I think about our clever outwitting of the unjust rules of our park. I am so glad we live in the country now, in rural Pennsylvania, where women still compete in the timing of their Monday laundry. A backyard clothesline filled with flapping laundry is a mark of respect around here, *thank God!*

Alex echoed, "Laundry?"

"Yep, and if you hand me those clothespins, I'll tell you a story about freeze-dried diapers."

Devin is a mature eight-year-old. He studied my face with skepticism.

"Is this a 'Once upon a time' story, or a *true* story, Grandma?"

I grinned. My reputation precedes me.

"Guess!"

They listened, their little faces rapt, fighting over whose turn it was to hand up a wooden pin. Even their father, our grandson, Dave III, the first of our family to wear Pampers, was intrigued by the olden days' story of the diaper dance, from pail to outside line. He did make a face and say, "Ewww," about the dirty diaper rinsed in the commode part

See why I love being a grandparent?

Cherish Every Moment!

❧❧❧

CHAPTER 33

Vicks, Goose Grease, and Mustard Plasters

B. P., (before penicillin), mothers of the 1940's and earlier used homeopathic remedies, also called *old fashioned cures,* to heal their families. Sicknesses ran the gambit from the grippe (flu), to bad colds, to pneumonia, and were treated with whatever happened to be available in the kitchen. My mother kept a shallow dish of melted goose grease on top of her gas range. If my sisters or I came down with the sniffles, we were ordered to bed and slathered up from chin to belly button with smelly, sticky, goose grease. To prevent stains on the bedding, a soft cloth covered the greasy mess. Often the ends of the cheesecloth were tied around our necks, cowboy style, to, *"Keep in the good."*

Skin cuts or open sores were slathered with Mercurochrome, and bandaged with gauze and medicinal adhesive tape. The Mercurochrome didn't sting, yet it smeared. Its bright red color leaching out of the edges of the homemade bandage announced to all our playmates that we were injured, maybe fatally! Otherwise, why would Mother use *real medicine* on our skinned knees or elbows? *Band-Aids,* those handy little strips of gauze and tape combined, an innovative new product put out by Johnson and Johnson, had not yet hit the marketplace. Some mothers in our neighborhood used Merthiolate as a disinfectant, but this new-comer in the home remedy department seemed to be shunned by the majority of our relatives. Maybe it was the unnaturally bright orange color that turned off the mother/healers? Whatever the reason, it never replaced good old (cheap) Mercurochrome in our family.

Yet, even after the wonderful convenience of *Band-Aids* hit our medicine cabinet, my mother could often be seen with blood soaked toilet paper wrapped around her cut thumb. She always cut herself after my father sharpened the kitchen knives. Some things never changed!

In my father's family, sick people were healed with mustard plasters, or the more potent onion plasters. This home remedy consisted of a double layer of cheesecloth, with sliced onions, and/ or hot mustard, sandwiched in between. Laid on the chest of the sick person, this potent poultice generated such heat that it was thought to, *draw out the germs.* Probably cooked them to death.

Sore throat? Bring out the hot toddy. Hot tea, with honey and a shot of whiskey, never failed to soothe a raw throat. Or maybe the alcohol-induced sleep cured us. Who knows?

By the time my baby brother entered the family in the mid 1940's, a miracle cure appeared in Mother's medicine chest. Vicks Vapor Rub, a blue jar of menthol rub, replaced the messier goose grease as a favorite cold remedy. This familiar blue jar has also remained a medical favorite for our big family. It still holds a place of honor in our medicine cabinet beside the spray antiseptic, the liquid bandages, tubes of antibiotic cream, and Band-aids of every shape and size. Children and grandchildren go through a lot of medical supplies. It pays to be ready for any emergency.

Cecile and brother Jimbo

Back in my childhood home, my little brother Jimbo suffered many illnesses as a baby. The first in our family to contact asthma, he wheezed his way through many a long night. The potent odor of Vicks seemed a permanent part of Jimbo's persona. The only problem? Vicks had to be rubbed on his chest, and my brother was intensely ticklish. Mother grew frustrated, tired of fighting with a wiry little boy who seemed all arms and legs as he tried to kick his way out of the nightly massage. In desperation, she turned to me. I had been babysitting my brother from the time I turned nine, and he did respond well to my touch.

"I give up!" Mother said one night. She glanced at me, watching from the bedroom doorway. "You rub his chest." She threw up her hands and walked away.

I approached my little brother. Fresh from his bath, he wore a white knitted cap over his head to prevent him from, *catching a chill* from wet hair.

Such a dear little guy, I thought, reaching for the blue jar of menthol rub.

"Now, Jimbo, you know I have to rub this on your chest, right?"

He nodded solemnly, his lips already curved into a grin.

"This is for your own good, Kiddo."

His grin widened.

I sat down on the edge of the bed and scooped up a big glob of Vicks. With one hand, I held one little arm down and went for the kill. My other hand snaked onto his chest and rubbed vigorously. Ever try to tickle a monkey's belly? Same result with my little brother.

"Oh ho ho ho ho," he laughed hysterically.

His arms and legs wrapped around my rubbing arm with surprising strength. The harder I rubbed in the Vicks, the tighter his legs and arms twined around my arm. All the while, he kept up his high-pitched laughter. We were both giggling by the time the chest rub was over. Even Mother, watching from the hallway, had to snort and chuckle. *Her darling boy.* She returned to the bedside with a soft cloth and tied it around his neck. I went into the bathroom across the hall and washed the smelly Vicks off my hands.

Just before I went upstairs to my bedroom and the waiting homework, I paused at my brother's bedroom doorway. The hall light fell upon his resting form, such a little mound in the big bed. Half asleep, his eyes gleamed in the reflected light from the hallway. Jimbo couldn't pronounce my name yet. He called me Cee-Lo, sometimes shortened to Lo, instead of Cecile.

"Good night, Lo," he said.

"Good night, Jimbo."

I'm sure missing you.

Cherish Every Moment.

CHAPTER 34

❧❧❧

Oddball Anniversaries
that End in Zero

(The sneaky tissue toss)

While living in California, Dave and I celebrated our fortieth anniversary. We decided to renew our vows at our church, St. Lawrence the Martyr. The pastor, Father Ryle, called us into his office to discuss the ceremony. He seemed unusually excited by the prospect of officiating at the renewal of our vows.

"Forty years!" he said, shaking his head and smiling. "Amazing! Wonderful!"

His astonishment that two people could stay happily married for four decades made us feel as if we had survived a nuclear war or something. He wanted to know everything about us. Where we met, how many children we had, grandchildren, too? *Wonderful!* His excitement seemed over the top.

It was many years later before I realized that in California, marriages seldom last that long. Anniversaries that end in zero are a very rare thing. People are free spirits out there in the land of sunshine, road rage and drive-by shootings . They marry (or not),

162

stay together as long as everything stays hunky-dory, but at the first sign of a problem, out the door they go!

In our neck of the woods, even if it is back-woods rural countryside (often an object of ridicule or the snide label: *Redneck territory*), married people stick together. Husbands and wives work it out, they endure. Since returning to our home state, we have noticed that an amazing number of married couples celebrate fifty, sixty, even seventy years of married life together. Each week, the local paper features an anniversary couple with a picture, either of their wedding day, or a recent photograph, and an article describing their family. To me, that spells security, a basic, decent, family-based morality. But in California, we were a rarity.

Father Ryle went all out. We were called up during Sunday Mass, arranged around the altar like the Apostles at the Last Supper. Our family stood behind us in a semi-circle.

Father began to speak (actually he raved a bit, I thought, squirming at all the attention).

"Pay attention, people. Here is a couple that is celebrating their fortieth wedding anniversary!" He smiled brightly.

I felt like a freak on display. Not my thing to be the center of attention around the altar of God. I squirmed, wishing it was over so we could return to the privacy of our pew. Then the actual renewal of vows began. I could concentrate on our pastor's words and forget the congregation of people staring at us. Across the far end of the altar, Dave glanced my way.

Uh oh!

Dave, the farm boy who grew up with the work-hardened muscles of a real tough guy, and whom nobody challenges when he is angry, is, at heart, a sentimental guy. His soft eyes were filled with tears and *his nose was running!*

Quickly, I reached up my sleeve for the tissues I always carry and passed them across the blessed altar of God to my runny-nosed husband. I don't think too many people noticed, but I did see Father Ryle grinning. He hesitated a moment, then went on with the ceremony. Afterwards, the entire congregation gave us a standing ovation. We have it all on video tape, and when I am feeling blue or neglected, I watch it again.

Life is good!

Cherish Every Moment.

CHAPTER 35

Our Electrical Ghost and Other Family Myths

After my sister, Joy, died of cancer in 1992, we noticed strange happenings in our California home. First it was The Bird.

Dave and I, our two dogs, Ginger and Sarge, were all sitting in our living room just past supper time one fine spring evening. Outside, audible through the screened windows, birds chirped and sang the ancient mating calls of their kind. A happy sound, tweety melodies to lift our winter-gray souls. We had lost my sister Joy to cancer in February. Eighteen months before that, my mother had succumbed to the same affliction. I, for one, felt weary to the bone from dealing with the painful losses of life. *Wish I felt like singing, like those silly birds out there,* I thought and heaved a big sigh.

One bird seemed especially loud, almost annoying in its persistent whistles and shrill cheeps. The sound grew louder. Dave rose from his recliner, peering over his glasses at a movement on the porch.

"There's a weird bird out there," he said, grinning. "It acts like it wants to come inside."

I got up to look outside. The silly bird *was* acting weird. It marched up and down the front porch, loudly complaining about something. Its colorful feathers ruffled as it continued to march up and down. It kept glancing at the screen door, loudly cheeping and whistling. On the top of her head *(had to be a female because she looked just like my sister Joy when she woke up cranky from her nap)* the multicolored, mostly gray feathers stood up in uneven spikes. Dave read my mind.

"The bird looks like your sister Joy."

I had to agree.

"Even sounds like her, that cranky croak in her voice toward the end, when she got mad about something."

The bird stopped marching and glared in our direction. Then she flew up and clung to the screen door with her sharp talons. Our dogs scrambled to their feet to bark dark threats aimed at the feathery intruder. The bird's complaints grew more shrill as the dogs bared teeth at her. I swear I heard my sister's voice as the bird glared directly into my eyes.

"A fine thing! I come to visit and you sic the dogs on me!"

Dave and I started to laugh. We pulled the dogs away from the screen door and reached behind us to shut the main door. As the thick door closed, the bird flew away, never to return.

But Joy came to visit many times after that, we believe.

My sister Joy had always enjoyed a good prank. April Fools' Day was her favorite holiday. Her jokes were legendary. She sewed her husband's pants leg together, across one leg just above the knee, in the leg that he always put on last. He stood, precariously balancing, one leg inserted into his work pants, the other leg struggling to fit into the rudely shortened pant-leg. While he danced and fell against the bed, Joy laughed herself silly. Another time she sewed her husband's fly closed on his underwear. Then one year, on the first of April, Joy snuck into our parents' yard and stuck plastic tulips into the snow in our father's pride and joy, his flower bed. When Pop noticed the overnight appearance of tulips blooming in the snow, he wanted to call the local newspaper and report a miracle. Good thing he called Joy first, or he would have been so embarrassed!

The year my father died, on April 1, 1968, put an end to Joy's April Fools' Day jokes, but did nothing to squelch her sense of humor. She took it to her grave and beyond.

The family had gathered for Joy's funeral in Florida. Dave and I came early since she wanted to say goodbye before cancer ended her life so prematurely. We arrived on Monday. Joy died the next morning while we were returning from the airport with another family member. As we gathered around her bed, weeping farewell to our oldest sister, the first inkling of our Joy-influenced future manifested itself. Much to the embarrassment of the Funeral Director, the hearse waiting in the driveway *refused to start.* The family, which included Joy's daughter Sue, hugged each other and shot long, sideways glances into each other's eyes. Mirth danced in Susan's eyes. Her lips quivered, not from grief this time, but from suppressed laughter.

She whispered into my ear, "Will we have to push-start Mom's hearse?"

Suddenly the ridiculous humor that surfaces whenever family gathers to mourn rippled around the crowded bedroom. Even Ed, Joy's husband, started to grin. The Mortician stared at us as the "grieving" family burst into loud laughter.

Thanks Joy, we needed that!

The next morning, while Ed made breakfast coffee, the kitchen radio sprung to life. No, it was not a timed appliance, it just burst into rock and roll music on its own.

"Joy's favorite song," he said and grinned. "She said she wouldn't leave me alone. Guess she meant it, huh?"

Later that day, the various television sets in the house began to turn on and off at will. Ed had made a living repairing television sets in earlier years. He worked most of the day, trying to solve the TV problem, to no avail. The appliances just seemed to have a mind (or *spirit*) of their own. After Dave and I returned to California, our television sets also began to "act up." Strange white circles danced across the screen of the living room set. The bedroom set refused to play VCR tapes one day, but worked fine the next day. The main television in the living room refused to be turned off, even after Dave unplugged it. Later, it worked fine. My computer crashed for no reason, then healed itself. The can opener buzzed on its own.

We were haunted, it seemed.

It soon became a family joke. Something wrong with an electrical appliance? *Must be Aunt Joy.* Similar things happened to other family members including a cousin who didn't even attend Joy's funeral! My sister makes our life interesting, especially in her birthday month, June, and the month of her death, February. We grin and bear it. Nothing like an electrical ghost to liven up your life.

Last month our puppy Smoky got into trouble with Aunt Joy. We had to leave the pup alone for too many hours while we traveled to a distant city for Dave's annual heart checkup. When we got home, we discovered a mess. Smoky must have decided he was abandoned and, being a hungry pup, took matters into his own paws. He managed to find the bowl holding his rawhide bones and ate several of them, paper and all. Then, perhaps bored or feeling vengeful, he brought down Dave's plastic place-mat, chewed off the corner, then went back and grabbed a needlepoint coaster and nibbled off a large hunk of it. *Uh Oh! Aunt Joy made that coaster!*

"Oh Smoky, you are in big trouble with Aunt Joy. I almost feel sorry for you, Puppy."

We didn't have to wait long for Joy's revenge. A few days later, I made waffles for lunch (healthy ones with oatmeal, honey, canola oil and blueberries). While cleaning up the kitchen, I swiped off the grids on the waffle iron and left it open to dry. It was nap time for everyone, so I headed into the bedroom. Dave relaxed on his recliner. Smoky faked a nap on his bed. Moments later a great commotion brought me racing into the kitchen. Thumping and bumping and squealing and yiiiiiiiiiiping and scrambling echoed through the house. When I opened the door to the kitchen, Smoky flew past me like his tail was on fire. Seems that the pup had crawled up onto the kitchen stand, stretched his nose to the waffle iron and *Whap!* It snapped shut on his face. He back-pedaled so fast, he fell off the stool and onto the floor, the waffle iron on top of him. Dave said the pup couldn't get his feet under him fast enough to escape.

"Told you Aunt Joy would get you, Smoky."

The pup hasn't been up on the kitchen counter since that day. Tough lesson for a mischievous dog. *Thanks Joy, we needed that.*

Cherish Every Moment.

CHAPTER 36

❧❀❧

Sarge the Wonder Dog

While living in California, we brought home a new pup to keep our old dog, Ginger, company. Ginger did not thank us, but spent her days glowering at the newcomer from the depths of her kitchen cave. The puppy, a spirited mix of Husky and neighborhood Romeo (we guessed his father might be a Doberman mix), kept all of us hopping. Stubborn and headstrong, he tried to dominate his house-mate Ginger. She did a lot of complaining, but eventually, they became partners in crime.

Newspapers ripped up? *"Sarge did it!"* Ginger insisted, whining and glowering at her best buddy.

Fuzz skinned off a tennis ball? *"Sarge did it!"* Never mind that Ginger had a long history of skinning tennis balls. When in doubt, blame the pup!

Hole dug in the corner of the rug? This time we knew Sarge did it. Ginger never dug holes, even as a puppy. As he examined the damage to our fairly new carpet, Dave ranted and raved at the puppy. "You ain't no friend of mine!"

This made me laugh, so I had to leave the room. No use trying to discipline anyone or any animal when I am laughing my

CHERISH EVERY MOMENT 171

buns off, right? Every one of my children and most of the grand-children realize that, if they can make me laugh, they get a free ride, a get-out-of-trouble card, no matter what they did. Dave repaired the damage to the rug with an extra piece of carpeting, but he muttered in anger the entire time.

"This is the last straw, Pup! One more thing destroyed and you are out of here!"

We talked about the mischievous puppy problem later, seeking solutions to Sarge's wild rampages. It always happened when we were out of the house for several hours. We tried to confine him to the kitchen, but he leaped over the wooden gate. Dave rebuilt it, higher next time.

He chewed the boards off until he could scale the gate once again. Once in the living room, he went wild, chewing and tearing up anything and everything in his path. Meanwhile, Ginger whined in the kitchen, too short and not adventurous enough to scale the gate with her partner in crime. We would come home to exhausted dogs. Ginger's voice reduced to squeaking from scolding, Sarge sleeping amid the remnants of his rampage. It didn't help that Sarge's antics made me laugh! *Cherish Every Moment.*

"Let's try something different, Dave," I said. "Let's forget the gate and just let both of them free to roam the living room. We can leave the television on so they hear people talking."

"I don't know ..." he said.

"Can't make it any worse, right?"

"Let's set up the video camera to see just what happens while we are gone," he suggested.

We gave it a trial run. One evening, we decided to take our usual walk, but we left the dogs at home. Before we left, we set up the camcorder on the kitchen shelf. An hour later, we returned to find nothing much disturbed in the living room. Ginger scolded us for leaving her alone again with *That Puppy!* But we found no de-

struction at all. We rewound the cassette and put it into the VCR.
What we watched on that tape made both of us laugh hysterically.

As soon as we walked out the front door, the dogs began to
play. Ginger did a lot of whining, but she kept grinning as Sarge
chased her around the living room. When she tired out, she headed
for her cave under the kitchen table. Sarge tried to nose her into
activity again, but no, the old lady was too pooped to participate.
Then things got really interesting. Sarge hopped onto the couch
and stared out the windows, his nose on the backrest, wistfully
waiting for us to return. After a bit of whining, he lifted his fine
pointed nose to the ceiling and began to howl. Not your ordinary
doggie howl, but a deep-throated, start in his toenails and reach
for the stars, wolf howl! We were astonished! We had no idea our
dog could howl like that. Never heard anything like it. When I
mentioned it to a neighbor later, she laughed.

"Oh, Sarge always howls when you guys leave."

Cherish Every Moment.

Ginger died a few years later and Sarge became our only doggy
companion. We cherished him beyond reason. He was friend,
companion, guard dog, and family comedian. He was so much a
part of our family that our grandchildren began to call us,
"Grandma and Grandpa Sargie."

When we moved back to East, he came with us and "helped"
as we built our house in the woods. He loved living in the country. Our neighboring farm dog, Fuzz, taught him to hunt, and
they had many adventures. Two dogs barking in the woods? Uh
oh, trouble thy name is Porcupine! Ever try to remove quills from
the nose of a one-hundred-pound dog that had a strong mind of
his own? Time for a visit to the Vet. While the dog was under
anaesthesia, the doctor discovered that his pancreas was enlarged.
Sarge died at age seven of pancreatic cancer. His death left us
bereft for many, many years.

Dogless, we helped care for Fuzz after his owners died. Every morning Fuzz came up through the woods, and accepted a hot dog, stuffed with a baby aspirin (for his arthritis). He came with me on my walks, until he became so lame that I tied him up when I walked to save him from pain. When new owners moved into the neighboring farm, Fuzz still came up for his hot dog. Sometimes he stayed overnight, sleeping on the rug on our porch. Other times he went down to his dog box on the farm. It hurt us to see him in such pain, but the new owners did not want to put him down. Then, during nap time one afternoon, I had a dream.

In my dream, I was looking out the kitchen window. Sarge stood outside just off the deck. "Sargie!" I said, "What are you doing here?" I realized, even in my dream state, that our dog was dead. I tried to call him into the house, but he tossed that proud head, and ran around the house. I watched from the living room window as he trotted down the dog path through the woods. He disappeared out of sight, heading for the farm, and his buddy Fuzz.

That evening, Fuzz's owner called. "Thought you might want to know, Fuzz died this afternoon."

I can see them both, running through the cornfields of doggy heaven. Just as they teamed up in life on this earth, one running through the corn, trying to shake out a groundhog, the other running alongside, waiting for the quarry to flush out. Good hunting, you good and faithful dogs.

Are there dogs in heaven? I sincerely hope so. Why would our loving Father give us these wonderful companion animals in life, only to deny us the pleasure of seeing our old friends again in heaven?

See you later, Sarge and Fuzz and Ginger.

Cherish every moment!

CHAPTER 37

Boys into Men

Little boys, gotta love them! Galloping through the house, knobby knees high, buttocks gleaming, wearing nothing but an oversized cowboy hat and fake gun belt.

"Hi, Pastor Smith! Jesus loves me just as I am!"

What is a mother to do but blush and laugh? No need to explain to the clergyman the true reason behind the nakedness of the boy. Even though most boys love to run around "in the buff," today is laundry day and his favorite green shirt and too-short-in-the-legs jeans are in the drier.

From the age of newborn until age six or so, depending upon the boy, little guys possess that winsome innocence that negates most of the outrageous behavior inherent in their species. Clinging to favorite clothing? Understandable. His grandpa does the same thing. Must be in the genes. Rather be nude than wear new clothes. Mud pies for lunch? Yum! Live frog in the laundry? Catch him before the spin cycle! Fistful of wild flowers crushed in a grubby fist? Bring out the best vase for his love offering.

Fast forward seventy years. Old man, shuffling through the house in his droopy boxers, his favorite tattered tee shirt, his slippers that flop at every stumbling step.

"Hi Pastor Jones, sorry I missed church last week. Couldn't find my car keys."

What is a wife to do but bite her tongue? The long-suffering wife knows that the old fart could have gone to church in her car, in fact she went alone and prayed for his soul! The stained and tattered clothes he favors embarrass her sense of house-wifely neatness. But he clings to them and raises holy hell if she dares to peel them off of him to toss into the laundry. Must be a guy thing, ya think?

What mean-spirited metamorphosis changed that winsome little boy into that cantankerous old man? It is a gradual thing, a coming of age type thing. Just as that little boy, around age seven, begins to lose his exhibitionism and actually don clothing to hide his nakedness, so does an elderly man revert to the same lack of inhibitions that served him so well as an innocent child.

The process begins around age seven, when a little boy suddenly discovers that the sight of his naked body is sometimes not appreciated by the general public. Maybe the startled gasps of Grandma or Aunt Betty lose the intended shock value, and his "flashing act" no longer seems appropriate. Maybe someone at school clued the little guy in, who knows? Suddenly the little nudist becomes a very private person, monk-like in his modesty.

"Mom! I'm taking a shower! No, I don't need your help!"

The yelps and general groaning convey the message: the little guy is growing up. No need for the mother to remind him, "I changed your diapers, young man. I know what you look like." Such reminders only make him more secretive.

"Mooooom! Shut the door!"

An older man, on the other hand, cares not what may be hanging out of his clothing. He leaves the bathroom door open and waltzes around in the nude. Maybe he is seeking reassurance that he still has all the normal male equipment, even if it doesn't work so well anymore? The mirror reflects a man, maybe that is all the reassurance he may need at that stage of his life.

The pure innocence and honesty of young boys is so appealing.

"You're getting fat again, Mom. Are we having another kid?"

My oldest son was correct. We were adding another child to our noisy household. When I nodded to his query, he said, "Hope it is boy this time. We have too many girls now."

At that point in time we enjoyed a family of two sons and four daughters. The newest child would be a boy, and three younger brothers would join the family in the coming years. Being the mother of a family of ten children, six of them sons, proved to be a daily adventure. Girls are wonderfully different than their brothers, sweet, eager to please, but prone to shrill giggles and dark drama. *"Nobody loves me!"*

Boys are rowdy, noisy, full of spirited energy, painfully honest, and up-front. Even their questions are to the point.

"Mom, if I break my arm, will I still have to help with the dishes?"

This creative slacker of *"girls' work"* is already eye-balling the tall pine trees visible out the kitchen sink. Another bite-my-tongue moment. To laugh is to encourage scenes of derring-do.

"Listen, young man, even if you break *both* arms you would have to help with kitchen clean-up. Remember our motto, 'no workee no eatee.'" This quote, of course, is a paraphrase from the *Bible*, St. Paul's second letter to the Thessalonians: *"... that if anyone was unwilling to work, neither should that one eat."* 2 Thessalonians, 3:10.

Our second son, Russ, a test-the-limits child who always had to learn stuff the hard way, actually did break both arms falling (or diving) out of a pine tree. And yes, he did continue to help with K.P. Rules apply to everyone in the family.

Something about little boys, gotta love them. Too bad they grow up too soon.

Fast forward fifty years. The darling children are grown and gone off to lead productive lives of their own (we sincerely pray). Now only Grandpa and I are left to do kitchen work. It is lunch time. After enjoying nice, healthy salads (Dave is diabetic), I tackle the big stack of combined breakfast and lunch dishes, washing them by hand as is our family custom. As an older woman, my body is not young either. My backbone begins to burn, a by-product of too many babies slung on my hip, too many years bent over the kitchen sink. I grit my teeth and work faster. The dish-cloth really spins as I struggle to outrace the inevitable.

At the table, Dave, raised by his old fashioned mother to dis-dain "women's work," is blissfully savoring his salad. I glance over my shoulder, projecting dark thoughts in his direction. Seems to me, the faster I work to finish the dishes, the slower he eats. Fi-nally, the burning turns to stabbing pain. I dry my hands, walk into the bedroom for the wide stretchy belt, lay a thin frozen ice pack onto it, and attach it to my waist. I really hate it when my back gives out on me. Makes me feel old, too-soon old. My heart is singingly young, but my body betrays me on a regular basis. Must be how Grandpa feels when he reverts to childish tantrums over the struggle to fasten his tiny shirt buttons. As if summoned by my sympathetic thoughts, he appears beside me, drying towel in hand, to help with the dishes. His mouth may still be chewing salad, but his heart is golden.

Old guys, gotta love them. Every older woman knows in her secret heart that she is statistically prone to outlive her husband. Even as we moan, complain, and roll our eyes when our boy/man/husband reverts to childish ways, we know that someday he may be gone and we will be left behind to mourn.

So we listen when God whispers,

"Cherish Every Moment."

CHAPTER 38

❧❧❧

Boys, the Middle Years

What is there about boys aged seven to twelve that makes them so much fun? Before they enter the teen years and the painful, slouching, sleep all the time, shower endlessly, phase, there is the wonderful tween time of boy stuff.

When we raised our family, I as Mother, found little time to enter into their robust games. But now we have thirteen grandsons of various ages, and I really enjoy their visits. The thumps above the kitchen mean boys bouncing, or wrestling, or building forts out of mattresses and blankets. They race down the steps, wearing blankets ripped off the beds as capes. They skip the last few steps in a vain attempt to fly like super heroes. Eyes of blue or brown sparkle, cheeks glow with excitement, knobby knees churn as they race past the breakfast table. There may be only two or three of them, yet somehow the sheer volume of their energy expands to announce the commotion of an advancing army. Out the back door, around to the front, up the steps again, the screen door slams, more thumps.

Grandpa, reading the morning paper, scowls darkly at the vibrating ceiling as if expecting to see a youthful leg protrude through the drywall at any moment.

"What are they doing up there, killing themselves?" But he grins, fondly remembering his boyhood and the exhausting games he played with his brothers and sisters.

"Boys will be boys," I say mildly and smile.

He shakes the newspaper and shouts at the ceiling. "Hey! Quiet down, up there!"

The wild yahoos and thumps quiet a bit, then go on a bit longer until the boys wear themselves out. When they exhaust that game (but not themselves), they slither down the steps on their bellies like crippled snakes and come to slouch against the kitchen counter.

"Grandma, wanna play cops and robbers?"

When I agree, it turns out they need a "bad guy," and I am chosen for this role because no one else wants to be bad. Bad guys miss out on the nightly ice cream ritual, which includes chocolate toppings and Cool Whip.

Grandpa is the first one to the table for ice cream each evening. He eyeballs each dish, measuring his bowl against the others to make sure he has a bigger portion.

"You boys better not be eating my ice cream," he threatens darkly.

"No, Grandpa, we know. You get the special sugar-free stuff. We get the good stuff."

"Mine is just as good as yours," Dave protests.

The boys grin. "Sure, Grandpa." Little diplomats.

Yet, no one wants to miss this nightly ritual by being bad during the day. I only eat ice cream once a week, hence, I am chosen to be bad guy in the cops and robbers game.

"OK, guys. I am the bad guy."

I am shackled by pretend handcuffs and ordered to sit in my walk-in closet jail. Plopping down on an extra case of soda, I begin moaning the old jailhouse song. "I'm in the jailhouse now ..."

The old song suits the occasion, but not the boys' sense of right and wrong.

The head jailor touches my hand. "You can get out of jail if you promise not to do bad again, Grandma."

"But I like it here," I protest and begin to sing again.

"Just say you're sorry, and you can get out of jail."

Reluctantly, I apologize. I *am* sorry the game is over.

"Hey boys? Want to go play in the creek?"

My suggestion revs them up again. Nothing like hot summer morning spent wading in the icy water, with tall green trees providing a cool canopy above. If we are lucky, we may catch an occasional glimpse of a curious deer. One boy, more timid than the rest of the rowdies, is worried about bears.

He asks me. "Why aren't you packing today, Grandma?"

He refers to the holstered pistol I wear on my daily walk through the woods. Bear sign, tracks, and waste piles, attest to the occasional presence of our larger wild neighbors. But I don't like to wear a firearm when the boys are along. My grin reassures the frightened grandson.

"You guys are making enough noise to chase away any bear within a mile!"

Reassured, he goes back to building a dam by dropping large rocks onto a spillway. Later we visit a frog pond. All of us are thoroughly muddy and wet by the time we break for lunch. We trek home, leaving muddy sneakers and clothes on the back deck to be hosed off by Dave, also known as Grandpa.

Some of the more adventurous boys linger on the deck long enough for Grandpa to give them a shot of the hose. Squealing, they tumble through the screen door and drip dry all the way through the house. The puddles are part of the price we pay for entertaining grandsons. No problem. Everything we own is wash and wear.

Dave's role as Grandpa is a mixed bag. He loves the boys, but their noise often makes him cranky, disturbs his afternoon nap, you know.

* * *

David

Actually, it is Grandma's nap that gets disturbed. But I know what do to then. Grandpa to the rescue.

"Get the berry buckets out, boys. Time to pick blackberries while Grandma takes her nap."

I load up the Quad with grandsons and old ice cream buckets. Their excited chatter echoes across the farm field as we putt-putt toward the berry woods. Grandma collapses into bed for an hour's nap. Entertaining boys can be exhausting, you know? Plus, my wife is not as young as she wishes she was!

* * *

Cecile

When Dave and the grandsons return, I am up and ready for a board game. Scrabble is a favorite. Teaches the boys their spelling and keeps my mind sharp. Most of the grandsons like Monopoly and they can play it without my supervision. It keeps them busy while I prepare supper. Dave warms up the grill for hot dogs, sausage and chicken. Boys are easy to please. Most of them enjoy kiddy food, what healthy eaters call junk food. White crackers (one grandson goes through an entire box while he is here for a weekend), macaroni and cheese (another boy existed on this dish for several years), garlic toast.

The grandsons have different treats when they live at home: Toaster tarts; sugar-sweetened cereal; lots of candy. But when they are here, we try to teach them healthy eating habits. Lots of fruit, fresh vegetables, whole grain cereal like oatmeal, wheat waffles or pancakes with sugar-free syrup. Part of it is the diabetic diet we live by so Grandpa doesn't go into insulin shock again. Part of it is the good habits of healthy eating we live by as part of retirement weight control. Boys don't care. If it smells good, tastes good, it is good! They inhale their supper, then leap up to bicker over kitchen duty.

"Do I have to make a chart?" I ask.

Guess so. I scribble initials on the calendar for different duties. Minutes later, after their fierce scrutiny ("It has to be fair, Grandma!"), the dishes are washed, dried, and put away. Weeks later I will still be hunting for the elusive bowl or kitchen utensil put away by a grandson in a big hurry to get outside and play baseball.

Baseball at our house is played with bats of different sizes and tennis balls. We do have regulation baseballs, but our yard is too small to contain some of the home runs the sluggers knock into the woods. Then too, a few of the grandsons have wicked arms and when they pitch the ball in my direction, I don't want to keep ducking all the time. I already wear permanent bruises on my hip from tennis balls flung seventy-miles-an-hour at me.

"Ouch! Jon!" I massage my hip and glare. "And you quit Little League? Why?"

His brother grins. "No control, Grandma."

Dave chuckles, and gets up from the deck chair.

"Give me that bat. I'll show you how to fire it right back at him. Maybe next time he won't try so hard to bean you."

The boys love it when Grandpa plays, too. His swings and misses are spectacular, so are his hits. We have to buy tennis balls by the gross now. Too many of them got lost in the neighbor's hay field. When the all balls disappear, it is bike riding time.

When the grandchildren were younger, we bought two small bicycles, two wheelers, in the twenty-inch tire size. One was blue, the other pink. Anna and her cousin Stephanie used the pink ones. The grandsons were smaller and fought over the tricycle, until they grew into the twenty inch bike. One grandson insisted on riding the tricycle until he was almost ten years old, even though he knew how to balance on a two-wheeler by then. We have four grandsons in the same age group and when they were all here on vacation, they shared the two bigger bikes until they suddenly became color conscious.

"Pink! That's a girl's color. I'm not riding a girl's bike, no way!"

This went on long enough that Dave and I began to shop for another boy's bicycle. We found it quite by accident one rainy Friday night. We had gone out to dinner and since we were in town, decided to pick up a few groceries. Usually on shopping excursions, we drive my car, the SUV, for its roomy interior. Easier to pack away the multitude of bags into my Ford Escape, than trying to squeeze everything into the trunk of his small sedan. But on this rainy evening, my car had just been washed and Dave wanted to keep it clean. So we took his car to town, had a delicious fish dinner, then went shopping for a few groceries at Walmart. He spent his time in the electrical department while I hit the produce aisles and picked up some milk. We met up in the main aisle outside the toy department.

On our way to the cash registers, something caught my eye. It was a wonderful throwback to earlier times, a retro-bike. Banana seat, coaster brakes, ape-hanger handlebars, the bike hung from a small display. Nice wide comfortable seat. No gears. Sharp looking. *On Sale*! Of course I had to have it. Grandpa got some amused glances from other shoppers as he wheeled it up to the cash registers. We paid for our purchases. He made me wheel it outside. As we entered the parking lot, a beautiful rainbow hung over the glistening cars below. I took it as a sign of approval, a heavenly grin, if you will, as I wheeled our new bike toward Dave's small car.

It began to rain again as we approached the car. We ducked our heads to keep our eyeglasses spot free and opened the trunk. Then the real fun began. Try as we might, we could not fit the

high handlebars into the trunk of the small sedan. He removed all
the junk he collects in his car trunk, folded down the back seat to
make more room, all to no avail. The wonderful bike just would
not fit into the trunk. Did I mention it was raining? Pouring actually. We stood there dripping, our bags of groceries floating gently
in the cart, rubbing our glasses to be able to see again, and scratch-
ing our soaked heads. What to do? It was a twenty-mile ride to
home.

"Maybe if I ride the bike beside your car? I could wrap one
arm around the door post so I wouldn't have to pedal up all those
hills? Maybe no one would notice in the dark and the rain?"

Dave snorted. "Your cap would fly off."

He put the back seats back into their normal position, and
moved the front seats all the way up as far as they would go. By
squeezing, sweating (despite the rain) and a lot of intense cussing,
he managed to jam the bicycle into the back seat and close the
doors. He drove home with his knees touching the steering wheel.
My hero! We chuckled all the way home.

Now, after Grandpa zooms all the tennis balls into the woods
and fields around our house, the boys still have two bicycles to
fight over. The old twenty inch one, and the new retro-bike.

As evening ends, and the boys wind down, Dave decides to
make a campfire. We have a stone-rimmed fire pit with plenty of
grass and lawn chairs surrounding it. I fetch the marshmallows.
The boys head into the woods to cut slender roasting sticks.

Is there anything better than sitting around a blazing campfire, happy eyes reflecting the sparks that float toward the dark
night sky? Noses in the air, the boys howl toward heaven, a raucous tribute to the beloved memory of Sarge. Why do scorched
marshmallows eaten right off the stick taste better than candy
bars? My heart swells as I watch the glow of happy youthful faces
as they dare each other to eat yet another sweet treat.

"I ate ten!" Bryan brags.

His brother Jon, older by four years, groans. "Barf-bag!" he says and sticks his index finger into his mouth.

Danny giggles. "I can eat more than ten," and proves it by loading his stick with four marshmallows at a time and setting them aflame.

Jon leans against my knee. "Grandma, are we still having ice cream tonight?"

Ah, to be so young and insatiable!

Cherish Every Moment.

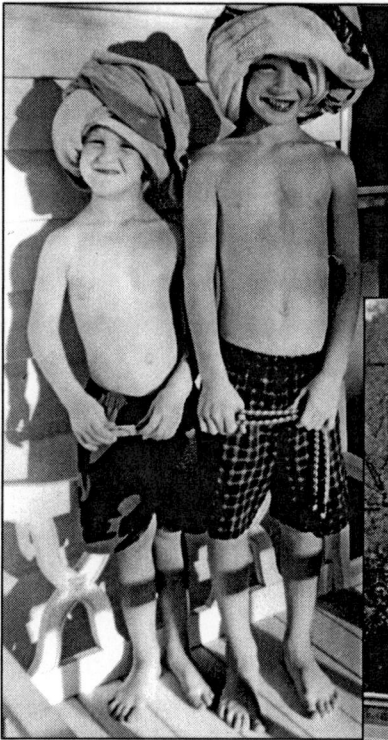

The Boys of Summer.

CHAPTER 39

❧

Girls into Grandmas

Although our clan seems top heavy with boys, we do have four granddaughters. The very rarity of their existence makes them so special to the entire family. Jackie, Cathy's daughter is a tall striking woman who has given the family two great-granddaughters, plus another great-grandson. Jennifer, Barb's oldest, is the mother of a boy. Stephanie, Mike's daughter, is in her first year of collage on a generous scholarship. Anna, Rose's daughter, gave birth last year to a little girl, Sierra Rose.

Anna is the granddaughter famous for her garlic toast. As a young teen, every summer she spent a week's vacation with us. As soon as she arrived, she headed for the bread drawer. Grandpa, walking into the house from the garage, would sniff the kitchen air and grin.

"Garlic toast! Anna must be here."

She loved visiting us in the wilds of Pennsylvania. Mornings would find her up early, romping in the woods with Sarge. Afternoons, she walked to our neighbor Sue's house and played with the assortment of grandchildren there. Sue is the designated baby-sitter for a large group of active little girls.

"I just love all those little kids," Anna often said.

She had the patience and good humor so necessary to deal with young children. She seemed programmed to be a Mom. Last year, Anna fulfilled her destiny. While living in North Carolina with her soul mate, Adam, she became pregnant. She telephoned with the wonderful news. I couldn't believe it, our little tomboy Anna to become a mother?

"Bet your Mom is happy, " I said during a pause in the conversation.

"I haven't told her, yet," Anna said and laughed. "I know you will keep it a secret, Grandma."

Touched beyond measure that she would call me first, I listened to her excited chatter over the long distance line.

"So when are you going to tell Mom and Dad?" I said.

"This weekend, when they are both home. I have a doctor's appointment tomorrow to be sure. Don't want Mom to get her hopes up if the pregnancy test is wrong."

We talked for a long time. I reassured her that both her parents, even her dad, would be thrilled to hear the news. Anna and her father always had a special bond. On the surface, this seemed like a good thing, except they tended to shut Rose, her mother, out of their relationship. I knew my daughter often felt left out of the loop when Anna and her father teased and laughed about their private jokes. Anna's pregnancy would change all that.

Amid the congratulations and giggling laughter, I paused to give a bit of sage advice.

"Anna, now that you will soon become a mother, you and your Mom will really be close."

"You think?" She sounded wistful.

So I was not the only one to notice that Rose felt left out of Anna's life!

"Anna, when you become a mother, you will suddenly realize just what a mother's love means." I laughed at an old memory. "In fact, my own mother told me the same thing. Grandma Ramier told me, 'It's only when a daughter becomes a mother that she starts to act human!' Funny, huh Anna?"

My granddaughter laughed uneasily. "I guess I have some bridges to build, huh, Grandma?"

"Your Mom loves you, Anna. Just remember that and let your heart lead you."

Eight months later, Rose and I drove down to North Carolina to be there for Anna when she gave birth. The long grueling drive seemed more than worth it as we hugged a very pregnant Anna and her excited Adam.

"Just think," he said, excitement tinging his deep voice, "Tomorrow, we will be parents."

The next morning we took two cars to the hospital. Adam planned to stay overnight after the baby's birth to be near his little family. Adam and Anna disappeared into the Birthing Suite. Rose and I waited in a huge room lined with chairs. As the long day crept by, ticked off by a large clock in the Waiting Room, the chairs filled up with families, also anxiously awaiting a birth.

It amazed me to see the large amount of family members all waiting for an addition to their family. Three and sometimes four generations gathered, greeted each other, exchanged progress reports, then waited.

Rose and I waited. We waited and waited. Occasionally, Rose walked back to the Birthing Room to check on Anna. The baby seemed to be in no hurry to arrive.

Every once in a while, a new father would appear in the hallway, holding a precious newborn bundle. All the chairs (except for Rose's and mine) emptied out as families leaped to their feet to greet the baby and its proud father. After this happy event, the chairs emptied as that family dispersed to their homes to share the good news. Rose and I waited.

Soon another pregnant mother arrived along with her extended family. The chairs filled up. People called happy greetings across the room. "Baby," seemed to be the most popular nickname. Didn't matter how old or young the kinfolk were, toddler or a great-grandparent, everyone was called, "Baby."

As in, "Paw-paw, have you heard anything yet, Baby?"

Paw-paw might be an elderly man wearing farmer's overalls, or suspender-clad jeans, which barely covered raw-boned skinny hips. His flannel shirt sleeves rolled up to reveal arms tanned to leather from working long hours in the fields. Yet he answered to Baby.

"Not yet, Baby."

To my northern ears, this drawled term of endearment sounded like, Bay-Bee. It fascinated me, the sheer size of the waiting families, and their obvious devotion to each other. Joy lit up every face as the newborn appeared in the hallway. The chairs emptied out.

Rose and I waited. Drawn with fatigue, my daughter's face mirrored her worry. I remembered the day I sat with her when Larry was born. Most grandmothers believe it is harder to watch and wait for your daughter to give birth, than it is to actually give birth yourself.

Finally, twelve hours after her labor began, Anna gave birth to a beautiful baby girl. Sierra Rose entered this world weighing a hefty nine-plus pounds (poor Anna!). Adam came out to get us. We flew into the Birthing Suite and cooed over this marvelous baby girl. As Anna dozed off, knocked out by drugs and exhaustion, Adam went out to grab a bite to eat. Rose and I sat beside the hospital bed. Rose, fighting tears, held Anna's hand. We both admired the baby, as the nurse checked her vitals.

"Want to hold her, Grandma?" the nurse said, holding out the swaddled baby.

Need she ask? I opened my arms to receive the precious bundle. Warm from the womb, a precious child of God, all the more welcome despite our long wait for her arrival. Rocking her gently, I sang her the same lullaby that welcomed all my newborns.

"Hush, little baby ..."

I glanced across at Rose. Biting her lips to keep back the tears, she stared at the baby in my arms. *This is not right. Rose is the grandmother, her very first grandchild!*

I stood up and walked around the foot of Anna's bed.

"Your turn to hold her, Grandma Rose."

Startled at the term, Rose choked back a sob and opened her arms. Instant love in a tiny pink bundle of baby passed from mother to daughter, great-grandma to brand new grandma.

Cherish Every Moment.

CHAPTER 40

꩜

Sierra Smiles

Later that week, while staying at Anna's, Rose and I had a mother-daughter quarrel. It left us both in tears. Why do adult women fight about unimportant things? Part of the problem began when a phone call home revealed that husband Dave had just been diagnosed with diabetes. His glucose level was off the charts. He had been trying to cope with a new lifestyle, reading labels at the grocery store, trying to choose healthy, sugar-free foods with no training in nutrition. I was wild to get home to his side. Then the stupid (on my part) quarrel. I felt terrible. Torn between my daughter's need to be with Anna who had such a rough delivery, and the very real danger of a newly diabetic husband eight hundred miles away, I pondered my choices.

We had driven down south with my car. Rose's car waited in our garage in Pennsylvania until we returned. If I took my car home to be with Dave, how would Rose get back? She had taken two weeks off from work to spend this quality time with Anna and the new baby. I just could not ask her to cut short her visit. Alone in the living room (Rose had retreated upstairs to be with Anna), I flipped through the telephone book, looking for car rental advertisements. One company offered to deliver the rental to your home. I put a bookmark in the phone book and dug out my credit card. When Rose came downstairs to fetch something for Anna's comfort, I offered a solution to our (actually *my*) problem. But first, I must apologize.

"I'm sorry, Rose, for hurting your feelings earlier. It was stupid of me."

She started to interrupt. I held up my hand.

"It's just that I am so worried about Dad. He's all alone in our house in the woods. What if he passes out? No one would even know about it until we go home next Sunday."

She gasped and looked worried, too.

"Here's what I think. You need to stay here with Anna. I need to go home. How about if I order a rental car for you?" I waved the credit card.

She sat down, shocked and blown away by the implications.

"You mean, you plan to drive home by yourself, Mom? It's a long trip."

She bit her lip. Rose is not an experienced long distance driver. Her legs go numb after a few hundred miles. Clearly she did not want to make that long trip alone, either.

"I don't know what to do, Rose. It's not fair to cut short your visit with Anna. But I am so worried about your father. Any suggestions?"

"Let me think about it, OK, Mom?"

I left her sitting and staring at the wall and went upstairs to talk to Anna. My granddaughter was sitting up in bed, nursing her precious little girl. Sierra was dozing, Anna was weeping. Incredibly, she blamed herself for the quarrel between Rose and me. She started to apologize.

"I know I haven't been very good company since we got home from the hospital. I'm up here all the time ..." she began.

As if her slow recovery from a difficult delivery had anything to do with my real worry about Dave!

"Oh, Anna, it's not that," I said, tearing up myself.

As I began to explain my problem about Grandpa's health, Anna swaddled up the baby in a receiving blanket and held her out to me. Nothing like the sweetness of a newborn baby as a peace offering. As I talked, Sierra squirmed. I glanced down once to see that those incredibly long legs of hers were kicked out of the blanket, again.

"Sierra, you silly girl," I cooed in baby talk.

My eyes ached with unshed tears, yet the baby warmed my heart. Little diplomat, she bridged the chasm between genera-tions with one generous act. Don't ever let anyone tell you new-borns can't smile. Because that precious little girl, barely a week old, gave me one of *my mother's* smiles! My mother had been dead for seventeen years, yet here was the genetic imprint of her un-mistakable smile, a gentle twisting of the lips, so well remembered from my childhood. My heart melted.

We worked out a solution to our problem later that evening. Rose called her son Larry and he promised to drive to Pennsylva-nia and spend the weekend with Grandpa. Relieved, I relaxed and enjoyed the rest of our visit with Anna and her new little family.

Rose and I arrived back at our house late Sunday evening. Larry helped us unload the car. Then he and his mother drove north to their Western New York home. On Tuesday of that week, Dave passed out at the lunch table. I sat beside him, waiting for the ambulance. My heart overflowed with gratitude as I thanked God *that I was home to call 911.* He spent an overnight at the hospital. Now his diabetes is in control again. We test his glucose every morning. He takes one pill a day, in the evening. Life is good.

Cherish Every Moment.

❧❀❧

CHAPTER 41

Johnny Two-Hat

John and Carole Smith had been our best friends for over thirty years. The friendship began at work (John worked with Dave), blossomed into family camp-outs, and grew into twice a month adults-only nights out. We attended square dances together, where the men really cut up on the dance floor. Sometimes, we met at each other's home and played cards. This couple had a marvelous sense of fun and we did a lot of laughing together. When Carole needed a job, I recommended her to my boss and we too became work buddies. We shared every family party with them and they reciprocated. First Communion party? Invite the Smiths. Graduation? Weddings? Any holiday party, we got together. Our families became good friends. They had five daughters, about the same age as our youngest five children, instant friends to hang out with. Some of our sons had crushes on the Smith girls, but sadly, it never came to anything serious. Even after Dave and I moved to the West Coast, John and Carole came to visit. We kept in touch via letters, phone calls and email.

After we moved back east to Pennsylvania, we spent an occasional day visiting them in Western New York. One visit, while

John and Dave talked about old times at work (both were retired), Carole and I took a walk. We sat down on a park bench within view of their house. She heaved a long sigh and told me her sad news.

"John is in the early stages of Alzheimer's Disease."

What do you say to comfort someone in this situation? Even best friends are rendered speechless, or prone to idiot speech by the shock of this most dreaded diagnosis, and the overpowering fear of the future.

"I wondered about John's speech ..." I said, my voice trailing away. "Thought maybe a mild stroke?"

Silly talk is not needed in times of heartbreak. God nudges us toward what is best in times of acute crisis. I opened my arms and we wept together. After a bit, I pulled away. Always, always, my practical side comes to the rescue. Stems the tears and the helplessness.

"So what are you going to do, Carole? Do you have nursing home insurance?"

She nodded and cleared her throat.

"The insurance is just in case we can't manage him toward the last." She straightened her spine. "But I intend to keep him home with me as long as I can. The girls and their husbands will help out."

I knew their family would do everything in their power to keep beloved John safely home with his loved ones. Wonderful family, and all of them lived within a ten minute drive.

Living with John as he struggled through that terrible mind-robbing disease did not alter Carole's finely honed sense of humor. As the years flew past, she related many hilarious stories about her Johnny. Grinning, she often said, "I have to laugh. Either that or cry all the time."

We visited as often as possible, making the three-hour drive north, staying for several hours, then returning home that same night. We usually had lunch together. I tried to bring dessert each time to ease the food prep for her. John's constant care left little time for Carole to fuss in the kitchen. Previously, she had loved to bake and cook. The multitude of Christmas cookies and the delicious care she invested in each culinary creation every December were, sadly, a thing of the past. Now all that took a back seat to the growing demands of her husband. Taking them out to a restaurant proved too upsetting to both of them. The last time we tried it, John started a food fight. He had slid into the pre-teen age by then, and his behavior was not acceptable in a family restaurant. Embarrassing for Carole, but his gleeful giggling made all of us laugh too.

"Don't encourage him," she said, but her laughter joined ours as he stuck straws up his nose.

One trip, I brought along a new recipe, a white chocolate/banana cake. We had purchased a new oblong cake pan for the occasion, planning to leave it with Carole. The cake tasted yummy. We all enjoyed it. John ate two pieces. After lunch, the men went into the living room to watch television while we women cleaned up the dishes.

"I have already lost so much of him," Carole said.

"I noticed that he is speaking less and less," I said.

Actually, he hadn't spoken at all the entire visit.

"Dave is good for him. I'm pretty sure he knows him," she said.

I realized that John no longer recognized me, but I said nothing. The puzzled look in his eyes, or rather the lack of recognition in his eyes, told me my identity was lost to John. His gradual decline made me so sad. His walking gate had deteriorated into a toddler's shamble. When John needed to go to the bathroom, Carole led him by the hand, a mother with a very large toddler. We could hear them in the bathroom.

"Wash you hands now, Johnny."

His reply was petulant, "I knooooow!"

But when they returned to the living room, both were smiling.

Cherish Every Moment.

Later that day, as we prepared to leave for the three-hour drive home, we stood in the kitchen doorway, hugging goodbye. Carole picked up the cake pan from the table.

"Here, don't you want to take the rest home?"

Before I could reply that we bought the cake pan for her to keep, John spoke up.

"No! I want it."

Keep in mind that he had not spoken a word to us the entire afternoon! His reply, *"No, I want it!"* made my day.

Cherish Every Moment.

John had a marvelous collection of baseball caps. They lined two walls of their laundry room. He had enough headgear to outfit several baseball teams. He had many favorites and often changed his cap to suit the occasion. Attending a Bills game? Have to wear the blue and red cap with the Buffalo emblem on the bill. Visiting us in Pennsylvania? Wear the Pirates cap. Going to a Jimmy Buffet concert? A parrot head cap, of course. Attending a Gaither Family concert? John wore a cap that said, *Christian under Construction.* He cherished his vast collection.

As his Alzheimer's progressed, John retained the love of his caps. In fact, some days, when Carole took him shopping (when no family member was available to stay at home with him), John wore two or three hats at a time. Owners of the local grocery store (a Mom & Pop store) grew to love Johnny's collection of headgear, too.

"Here comes Johnny-two hat," they said and smiled as Carole and John walked through the door.

Carole and John Smith

John would touch his caps and grin. Carole, of course, would crack up. They loved to laugh. She cherished him until the end, caring for him at home, with the help of their large extended family. When God called him Home, his coffin was lined with, what else? Baseball caps!

Cherish Every Moment.

CHAPTER 42

Carole, Grace Under Fire

A few months after John died, I heard from Carole via email. She had been oddly quiet for several long months, but I chalked it up to the inevitable numbness of a new widow. I kept in touch by sending email messages, e-prayers and an occasional *thinking of you* greeting card via snail mail. I am not your typical telephone chatterbox, almost expected in women my age. Instead, I prefer the written word to keep in touch. One day, after sending another long chatty email message to Carole, I received her reply.

My heart skipped a beat as I began to read.

Sorry it has been so long since I emailed you. Been kinda busy. Had some chest pain and when they did an X-ray, they found a suspicious lump in my chest wall. Having a Cat Scan tomorrow. Let you know later. Love and prayers, Carole.

Stunned to my core, I shut off the computer without replying. Later, after many tears and a long sleepless night, I returned to email a carefully crafted answer to Carole's shocking message of the day before. Before I could reply, another message from Carole awaited.

Doctors say it is stage 3.5 cancer. I begin chemotherapy next week. Pray for me.

If prayers could have saved Carole, she would be alive and well today. But God had other plans for her. Within a year, she reunited with her beloved John.

But during those long eleven months, we were continually surprised and gratified to realize that Carole did not suffer her terminal illness with a gloom and doom attitude. She was an example of grace under pressure, continuing to laugh and joke with her devastated family. She made it a point to live as normally as possible. Between her chemo induced weeks of nausea and weakness, she graciously carved out time to spend with us. We went out to a restaurant for lunch and she sported a spiffy yellow scarf to hide her lack of hair. It matched her pretty flowered summer dress and highlighted her wonderfully sunny nature. Knowing her sense of humor, I sent her joke gifts to make her laugh. A bouquet of flowers for her birthday included a pinwheel and the unsigned note, *from your greatest fan.* The fan reference was an old private joke between our two families. It took her a while to figure out who sent the flowers, but when one of her daughters solved the mystery, Carole called immediately.

"You crazy lady!" she said and exploded in laugher. We talked for a long time, a record phone conversation for me. As she said goodbye, she whispered, "You have no idea how much I love you two."

That marked the last time we spoke. She is with her Johnny now, laughing and joking and happy for all eternity.

Cherish Every Moment!

CHAPTER 43

Smoky, the Long Necked Pup

"The woods are lovely, dark and deep, and I have a pup to walk before we sleep."

Apologies to Robert Frost.

Seven years after Sarge died, we finally started looking for a puppy. The house was too lonely, especially in the winter time when few of the grandchildren or our adult children ever visited. Dave, now diabetic and arthritic, needed his exercise, but the recliner held him captive most of those long dark winter days. In the summer, he got his "exercise" by riding the lawn mower or the Quad. I did my daily mile walk, but then spent entirely too much time closeted away in my office, not doing productive writing, but playing video games. We needed a shake-up call.

The summer of 2007, we began our puppy hunt at the local Humane Society. The first visit, we looked at lots of dogs, but none tugged at our hearts. One dog resembled Sarge, but he was already six years old. We feared losing another animal too soon. Good dogs never live long enough. Not only that, a dog that looked

like our beloved Sarge, would not *be* Sarge. We might be fooled
into false expectations, and we would be miserable if this grown
dog did not live up to our cherished memories of his predecessor.
At our age (both of us are in our seventies), we didn't need more
heartache in our lives. Disappointed, we walked away. A week
later we tried again.

This time, a pup caught our eye. He was dark brown, with a
Labrador's ears, and soft hopeful eyes. He had huge paws and
promised to become a big dog someday. He cried and cried as we
took him outside for a walk. After a bit he stopped whining and
snuggled into my arms.

Sold!

Bringing a puppy into our settled lives sure changed our dull
and boring routine. We needed to pup-proof our house. Shoes,
boots, anything chewable had to be put up and out of the reach of
itching jaws. The snarl of wires behind our living room television
set-up had to be blocked by a sheet of plywood to keep them (and
the pup) safe. No more vegging out in front of the television or
playing endless video games. Pup needed a walk. *Now!* No more
sleeping in every morning. Pup whined at the bedroom door at 5
a.m. He needed a walk. *Now!* No more staying up late watching
the same old, same old, reruns on TV. By nine o'clock, we all
headed for bed, exhausted after being up since five.

Because I can move more quickly than Dave, it became my
responsibility to leap up when *Now!* threatened. Smoky and I became well acquainted with our woods. He loved the fiddle-head
ferns, running through them, letting their lacy tips stroke his sleek
back. It often triggered his elimination process. I would stand and
stare around the vivid greenery, inhaling the deep woods' scent of
bark, humus, leaf-mold, plus the occasional droppings of a wild
animal. Had to watch Smoky closely because if he found the droppings of deer, he gobbled them up. Yum, tasty! He also loved wild

mushrooms, or toadstools (can't tell the difference). We had a wet summer that year and the mushrooms bloomed everywhere. I had often wondered if they were the good ones, edible, or the poisonous types. They didn't seem to hurt the pup, but I still picked every one I found and tossed them into the trash.

On our excursions into the deep woods, I developed a new and keen appreciation for our property, and the natural wonders that I had overlooked before. What beautiful trees! Such vivid colors in the ferns. How tasty the blackberries were that year. Smoky picked and ate the berries on the lower branches, despite the thorns. Dave and I picked the upper ones and enjoyed them on our cereal.

It seemed a magical time, the woods' walking, the funny antics of the pup, tripping over his big paws, tumbling onto his back, feet waving in the air. His fierce charges, yipping all the time, at the birds. Smoky couldn't seem to figure out where they went when they disappeared into thin air. His expression of puzzlement made us laugh. In fact, most of what he did made us laugh. God knew we needed a puppy and God provided the perfect dog for us. Thank you, God, for your kindness and love.

Cherish Every Moment.

As Smoky grew older and larger, he began to accompany me on my long walks. I take the walk-path on the edge of the corn fields, skirt the woods for a half mile, then turn around at the top of the farm field and head back. At first, the pup would only walk just so far away from our house. As long as he could see the roof line of our house, he bounced along, happy for the walk. But when all familiar buildings disappeared in the curve of the fields, he high-tailed it home. Smoky has never been the bravest pup in the world. After a week or so, his short legs grew long enough, and he grew courageous enough, to dance along beside me the whole way to the top of the hill. I could tell he was proud of himself by the way he pranced, head high, tail wagging, tongue lolling as he surveyed the country-side. *Corn stalks? Yum!* He tackled them, pounced them into submission, and teethed on the leaves. As the corn grew tall, he became brave enough to weave his way through the rows, eyes sparkling, alert for adventure.

One bright summer morning, we were out walking before 7 o'clock. I wore my pistol, as usual. Coyotes love young pups, eat them for breakfast. As I strolled up the final hill, I noticed two young deer up ahead on the walk-path between the corn stalks and the woods' line. They stood in bright sunlight, nibbling on the grass beside the path. I stopped, waiting for the pup to catch up with me. Crouching down, at pup level, I grabbed Smoky's harness and held on. In this area, dogs who chase deer are often shot by hunters. I did not want Smoky to learn to chase deer. We crouched together, Smoky and me. Ahead, the deer were staring in our direction. The biggest animal began to walk toward us.

Young and dumb, I thought. Our term for deer too young and too foolish to beware of humans. Beside me, Smoky stared around, wiggling. He had not yet spotted the deer approaching us. I took his head and turned it toward the deer, now about fifty feet away. I pointed.

Suddenly Smoky's neck stretched high. I swear it grew an extra three inches as the pup took his first long, frightened, look at a wild animal, a big wild animal! *Zoom!* My arms emptied out in a big hurry. Smoky headed for home, ears back, legs churning, tail down as he zipped down the path on a dead run. I laughed silently. No worry about that pup chasing deer!

Ahead, the deer walked closer, its neck stretched toward me. I had my pistol, I could have brought home some illegal meat. Even a poor shot like me couldn't have missed at that distance. But it was not deer hunting season, and besides, I don't like to shoot young and dumb animals. If the deer had charged, or if it had been a coyote or bear, I would have brought out the pistol. But this was merely a curious young deer, too inexperienced to sense danger.

I cleared my throat. "Bang, bang, you're dead," I said. "Take your friend and go to bed."

To my amazement, the deer listened politely to my bad poetry, then turned leisurely, and strolled back into the woods. I continued my walk up the hill, then turned to go back home. Bright sunlight blinded me. I realized then that the deer had not been able to see either Smoky or me in the deep shadows of the walk-path. No wonder they weren't alarmed by the sight and sounds of a human or a frightened pup.

Young and dumb, long may they live to astonish another walker in the woods.

Cherish Every Moment.

❧❀❧

CHAPTER 44

Stinky Feet

From the time I met Dave, and really began to spend time with him, it seemed very noticeable that he had a foot odor problem. In plain words, he had stinky feet. He blamed it on wearing a pair of sneakers as a boy, sweating into the rubber material until his feet reeked.

"Those sneakers," he claimed, "they ruined my feet forever."

Well when you are in love with a great guy, you take the good with the not so good. So for years, we dealt with his foot odor problem. He insisted that cotton socks were the only type he could wear, and I made sure he always had white cotton socks. In the summer, when heat and humidity made his feet sweat, he used Absorbine Jr., an over-the-counter liquid which seemed to keep the burning and itching at bay. But he never found true relief, until our son, Mike, returned from serving in the Army. He moved in with us temporarily in California, and clued his dad into what worked for the Army.

"There were lots of guys with problem feet, Dad," he explained. "All that marching, those heavy combat boots, boy, when it was lights-out time, the stink from all those sweaty feet knocked us

out right away!" He paused, then continued, "Of course, sometimes, after a twenty mile hike, the smell was so bad it kept us all
awake, gagging and puking!" He chucked at the memory.

Mike held out a can of spray powder. "Here Dad, try this.
Works for the Army. Should work for you, too."

The miracle spray was Tanactin, and by golly it did work. No
more smelly feet for Dave.

Until he had the septic tank accident, that is.

We were living in our retirement home by then, in the woods
of Pennsylvania. Far from city water and sewer hookup, we had a
drilled well, and our own septic system. This consisted of double
septic tanks, plus a sand mound, all approved by the local Department of Environmental Protection. The first tank held a submerged
pump that pumped the liquid from that tank to a second tank. I
never understood the how or why of it, but the men in the area
seemed to know just how things like that work.

One fine summer day, the submerged pump quit. An alarm
went off down cellar, part of the early warning system installed by
Dave and our nephew, Butch. I was home alone at that point and
didn't have a clue what was happening. Did the tank need to be
pumped? Some electrical part need replacing? What?

When Dave got home, he knew immediately what to do. After lunch, he cleared the ground off the cover to the first septic
tank, pried off the concrete cover, and using a rope left on the
pump for just such emergencies, he fished out the submerged
pump. With our hose, he rinsed off the gunk, and used a testing
tool to discover that the pump was ka-put. We took a trip into
town and bought a new submergible pump, plus a new concrete
cover for the hole, since Dave had cracked the old one prying it
off with a crow bar. Now the fun began.

Dave's brother John came over just then for a visit. He and
Dave set to work, hovering over the opening to the tank despite

the potent fumes drifting up from the uncovered septic swill. They were hard at work on the electrical wiring, changing wires from the old pump to the new one, when I left for my daily walk. A half hour later, on my return, things had taken a definite turn for the worse in the smelly feet department.

Brother John was laughing. Dave was blushing with embarrassment and irritation. And one of his shoes definitely had a new odor de phew!

"What happened? Can't I leave you two alone for a half hour without someone getting into trouble?"

John chuckled. "Dave tripped and fell into the septic tank."

"Well, I didn't do it on purpose! I tried to step over the hole to get a tool and I tripped."

John turned to me, and wiped his eyes. Whether from laughing so hard, or the ripe odor, I couldn't really tell.

"You should have seen it, Ceil! He did the split. One foot into the hole, the other one on top." He swiped his eyes again. "And I couldn't even help him. You know how my back is."

I did know. John had suffered two back surgeries in the past few years. No way he could have yanked his bigger brother out of any hole, let alone the septic tank hole.

John chucked again. "I thought about hooking him up with a rope to the Quad and dragging him out like a stuck cork in a bottle."

Somehow Dave had managed to lift himself out of his predicament. He was hosing off his shoe as we watched. I went into the house to get a clean sock for him. I tossed the old one in the burn-barrel. Wished I could have also dumped his smelly shoe but it was a very expensive, custom-made work shoe, and no way could we waste money like that.

I cleaned it up the best I could, sprayed it every day with fabric deodorizer, and still the smell made our eyes water. For a few weeks, the shoes stayed outside on the front porch at night, a gentle reminder of our not so fond memories of Dave's stinky feet days.

Cherish Every Moment.

CHAPTER 45

The Rise

In 2001, a member of our extended family died, my sister-in-law, an aunt to our adult children. Whenever there is a death in the family, the clan gathers. Because the Wake and funeral came in the beginning of July, which has always been the traditional vacation time for our family, our little house in the woods bulged with people from several states. All the company beds were filled. Several nearby relatives opened their homes for the overflow, and still we had youngsters sleeping on the floor. As is the custom in the country, people brought food. Our kitchen and the basement refrigerators and freezers were stocked with enough food to feed our small army of kin for a month.

The first evening's Viewing was well attended by most of the adults in our family. The next afternoon, I volunteered to stay home to supervise the kitchen, plus take care of the grandchildren too young, or too *unwilling*, to visit the funeral home. Jonathan, nine, our youngest son's boy was among the unwilling.

"I'll go to the funeral, Grandma, but I don't want to go to the *rise!*"

"The rise? What do you mean, Jon?"

He clamped his lips together firmly and turned away, avoiding my puzzled stare.

"You know, Grandma," he said, hanging his head as if ashamed of his fear, "I don't want to see any bones."

It took me a while to pry it out of him, but the misinformation came from his religious education. Both Jon and his younger brother attend Catholic school, where daily Scripture Study is part of the curriculum. Seems his class had been discussing Ezekiel, Chapter 37, The Vision of the Dry Bones.

"The hand of the Lord ... set me in the center of the plain, which was now filled with bones... How dry they were!"

After a bit of discussion with the Lord, the prophet is urged to, "Prophesy over these bones... See! I will bring spirit into you, that you may come to life."

The part that spooked Jonathan must have been verses 7 to 10: "... even as I was prophesying I heard a noise; it was a rattling as the bones came together, bone joining bone. ...they came alive and stood upright."

In the vivid imagination of a nine-year-old, going to view a dead body (he pictured skeletal bones) who might sit upright and come to life was too scary to even think about. Nightmare time.

That afternoon as a huge meatloaf warmed in the oven, I sat down with three of the grandsons, Jon, his brother Bryan, and Danny, Larry's brother, and explained about funerals. They would all be going to the funeral tomorrow with their parents and I didn't want any terrified children howling in fear as the coffin was rolled down the center aisle of our little church.

"It will be very much like a regular Mass, boys, only there will be the coffin up front. It will be closed, so you won't see the dead body."

I nudged Jon, and even as he blushed, his expression showed relief.

"Funerals are sad time for the family, so people will be crying. Even grown-ups will be crying, so don't be surprised."

Bryan, age five, piped up, "Will they have to go to the cry-baby room?"

I wondered briefly how much time Bryan spent in the Bawl Room, as our pastor labeled it.

"No, adults don't howl out loud when they cry. They just have tears running down their face. Quietly," I said firmly.

"Oh."

"Then after the Mass, we will follow the coffin out to the cemetery. Our pastor will read some prayers of comfort for the family."

"Will we get to see the hole in the ground?" Danny asked, his blue eyes very wide with anticipated horror.

I sighed. "No, the hole, the grave, is usually hidden by a green rug so the family won't be more upset. Just thinking about their loved one going down into the earth is pretty upsetting to some people. But we Christians know that it's only their body, not their soul, going into the earth."

All three boys looked relieved. Although, as young boys who loved to dig in the dirt, I believe they all, secretly, wanted to see the deep hole. My hunch proved correct, because the next morning, all three boys begged their parents to take them to the nearby grave to see the *deep hole.*

After a long pause with no more questions, I concluded.

"And that's it. After the prayers at the grave-site, we go down to the social hall and have lunch. They call it The Mourners' Brunch around here. The ladies of the church put it on."

"How much does it cost?" Bryan is the practical one.

"The Brunch? It's free, a service of the church."

"Will they have chocolate cake?" Dan asked.

"Probably."

"Cool!"

Ah, sweet-loving, hungry little boys. As long as there is a promise of chocolate cake, all is well.

Cherish Every Moment.

CHAPTER 46

Mother's Rhubarb Stash

In my earliest childhood memories, beer played an important part of everyday life. My parents were social people who often held card parties and hosted numerous family gatherings. My dad favored a double hooker (two shots) of Canadian Club or CC, with a beer chaser. Local people in the Buffalo area called that combination a Lackawanna Boilermaker, named perhaps for the hard working men in the steel mills.

My mother preferred her beer straight from a tall brown bottle. No hard liquor, thank you very much. Genny Cream Ale remained her personal favorite.

As the years passed, and after my father died, Dave and I became the party givers. At our family celebrations in our country home, Mother always brought along her personal supply of beverage, just so she wouldn't run out, you understand. My middle sister and her husband, Betty and Len, usually brought Mother with them, so she didn't have to drive those long thirty miles home, and maybe risk a DUI ticket. Once they arrived at our party, Len unloaded the trunk of his car. Betty always brought along her special meat dish, Wimpies, a hamburger dish in a yummy sauce.

Mother brought her famous baked beans, made in a green crock that always seemed to make those beans taste so special. She also brought her beer, of course. The last thing unloaded from Len's car was a brand new beach ball. Mother loved playing Kick-ball with our kids. As soon as they arrived, the party began in earnest. Mother opened the first of her long-necked bottles. Betty put the Wimpies on the stove top to heat up, and the beans went into the oven. By the time the food was hot, Mother was on her second or third beer. Busy with the serving of my potato salad and Dave's grilled hot dogs, I assumed that she only drank one beer before eating. But after the party, the kids told me that Grandma always hid her empties under the couch.

"So Joy won't yell at me."

Joy, my oldest sister, had appointed herself the conscience of our family, after our father died. She insisted Mother needed someone, "To keep her straightened out." But that was just Joy. The rest of our family had no problem with Mother's drinking.

After our sumptuous picnic, Grandma brought out the kick ball and the kids went wild. I have a treasured home video of my mother, as she waited her turn to kick the ball and run to the nearest tree (first base). Dressed in pedal pushers and dark top, her arms wild and flapping as she listened to some inner music of acute happiness, Mother danced with wild abandon. The smile on her face told it all, *Cherish Every Moment.*

During this same picnic, while walking from our house to the back yard festivities, Dave noticed something in my rhubarb patch. He caught a glimpse of something shiny. He parted the large umbrella-shaped leaves and peered in to the deep shade.

"What the heck?"

Dave brought out three full bottles of Genny Cream and waved them gently toward Mother, now on the pitching mound. Mother slapped both hands on her knees in a gesture of resignation.

"Oh, you found my stash."

She didn't even have the grace to blush!

This became a treasured family story. *Grandma's stash* always brings laughter and fond smiles when we mention it. Today, in my rhubarb patch, I keep three or four brown bottles (empty of course), just for old time's sake, and to honor her memory. It seems to promote good growth in those tall stalks, source of such good pies and sauce. Whenever I share a shovel-full of rhubarb stalks with other gardeners, I tell them the secret of my ample crop. "Keep brown beer bottles among the leaves. Works for me."

Widowed at an early age, Mother lived alone for twenty-three years. Every night, as she watched the evening news on WBEN, she drank two servings of her favorite brewski before hitting the bed. She claimed it helped her sleep. Dave and I had no problem with Mother's drinking habit, but it drove my oldest sister, Joy, wild.

"A woman her age shouldn't be drinking every night!" Joy often complained to me.

I tried patient reasoning with my bossy sister. Might as well have talked to the wall.

"Mother is free, white and over twenty-one. She doesn't hang out in bars or pick up men. She doesn't get drunk and drive. She gave up her driver's license ten years ago. What she does in the privacy of her own home is *her* business, not ours," I said, more than once.

Joy persisted, "But she's getting older (later this changed to, *she's over eighty now*). What if she falls down the cellar steps and breaks a hip or something?"

It never happened. Joy's nagging complaints never changed, either. What changed was that a case of the long necked bottles of Genny Cream became too heavy for Mother to lift and carry home in her little shopping cart. She switched to twelve packs of canned beer. She also changed her method of hiding the empties.

One summer's night, Dave and I were back East on vacation, visiting our adult children and their children. We slept at Mother's house since none of our family had a spare bedroom. The three of us had played cutthroat Pinochle all evening. At bedtime, we said our good nights and turned to climb the stairs to my childhood bedroom. Mother sat in front of the television.

"Guess I'll just watch the news," she said. "Sleep tight, you two."

Dave had a little trouble getting used to a narrower bed. We slept in a king sized at home. He tossed back and forth a few times, then settled into a doze. Light snores escaped his lips. I started to drift off, when a commotion startled us both wide awake.

Clang, clang, clang!

"What was that?" Dave said, bolting upright, eyes wide and staring.

Again a loud clanging echoed up the stairway from the downstairs bathroom.

Dave tossed back the covers. "Better check on Grandma, she might be hurt or something."

I touched his arm and started to giggle. A memory of my baby brother surfaced, the way he used to toss his fleet of Tonka trucks down the laundry chute just to hear them rattle their way to the bottom. Then he would point and wail, his little bow mouth in an upside down smile, until one of us trekked down to the basement to rescue the trucks. Jimbo would wait, his blue eyes wide with expectant joy, as Mom or Dad or me would reach up and unfasten the door of the clothes-chute. A flutter of dirty garments, and an entire fleet of toy metal trucks and cars came tumbling to the basement floor. My little brother would clap and crow. He never tired of the game. Now, forty years later, in my childhood bed beside my alarmed husband, I recognized the tinny rattle of the clothes-chute.

"Mother is all right," I said. "She's just getting rid of the evidence."

"What?" Dave turned to me, frowning.

"Remember Grandma's stash? The empties under the couch?"

He sank back onto the pillow and grinned. "She throws the empty beer cans down the clothes-chute?"

"Yep!" We giggled about it for a half hour before we finally went to sleep.

The next morning, I approached my mother. "Do you mind if I do some laundry today? Nice sunny day. I can hang the stuff outside."

I kept my face carefully innocent as I hurried down the cellar steps, carrying an armful of dirty underwear and socks.

Mother hurried over to her washer and turned on the water. *Perfect!*

"I don't have enough for a full load, Mother. What do you have that needs washing today?"

Before Mother could stop me, I reached above my head and opened the trap door that emptied the contents of the clothes-chute onto the basement floor. *Clang, clang, clang!* Empty beer cans rolled in every direction. I turned to Mother, unable to control my laughter. This time she did blush.

She flapped both hands on her knees in that familiar gesture of embarrassment.

"Oh, I never could put anything over on you, Cecile!" she said and laughed.

Another treasured story the whole family cherishes.

Last week I dreamed about Mother and Joy. Both have been gone from this earth since the early 1990's. In my dream, I stumbled into a family-type bar room. The floor looked like rough wooden planks and it must have been an old establishment, because the floor slanted to one corner. I stumbled as I crossed the threshold and ordered a drink. Joy was bartender, and as every good bartender knows, you don't serve a customer who seems visibly drunk. She had no qualms about refusing to honor my drink order.

"No," Joy said in that bossy tone so familiar from my childhood. "You are staggering already. No drink for you tonight."

Outraged, I began to explain that I have Benign Positional Vertigo (true) and besides, her floor was slanted. "Who wouldn't stagger in this place?" I demanded.

Before Joy could answer, I noticed something else astonishing about the scenario. My mother sat at the end of the bar! Mother, whose lady-like form never graced the inner sanctum of any bar, especially a cock-eyed one like Joy's Place, sat on a bar stool. In front of her, sat a tall brown bottle of Genny Cream. As I watched, mouth hanging open in astonishment, she raised the bottle and took a long (definitely unlady-like) slurp.

"Mother? What are you doing here?" I asked.

For the first time in seventeen years I heard the beloved echo of my mother's stern voice in my mind.

"Enjoying myself!" she retorted.

I can't stop grinning.

Apparently, despite the old polka tune, in heaven, there *is* beer. Raise a foamy glass with me as we toast an unquenchable spirit.

"Here's to you, Mother. Enjoy yourself for all eternity!"
Cherish Every Moment!

My mother, enjoying herself.

❧

CHAPTER 47

So This is Paradise

In the late 1990's, not long after we built our house in the woods of Pennsylvania, the church we joined, St. Mary's of Crown, decided to put out a Parish Directory. Because I worked in the rectory office as Assistant to the Secretary, I became Committee Chair in charge of the telephone list. Parishioners were encouraged to sign up for designated dates and times to have their portrait taken by Olan Mills. My job was to call and confirm their choices, and also remind each family of the time and date of their scheduled photo slot. As Contact Person, my phone number was given to the photographer and other sales representatives. This meant a lot of time spent on the telephone, not my favorite way of communicating.

I really try to avoid talking on the phone, an old phobia from the telephone calls received from my sister Joy. My oldest sister never called me, never. The exception being to share with me the tragic news of another death in the family. Every time the phone rang, and I knew I had to answer it, my heart thudded with dread.

Oh no! The phone is ringing. Has to be bad news!

So with this assignment of Telephone Committee Chair, I had to force myself to be professional, and *talk on the phone for heaven's sake*! I looked upon it as a sort of penance, a peace offering to God, an atonement for my many failures in life. It never got any easier. When the phone rang one day, I picked it up with the usual dark dread hammering in my throat.

The voice on the other end, a young man, sounded as uneasy as I felt.

"Ummm, this is Dave Peters," he said and gulped.

"OK," I said, and waited.

If this guy is a telemarketer, he needs more training, I thought.

"Ummm, I am the photographer for Olan Mills."

"All right," I said with a bit more warmth in my voice.

"I am new to this area. Do you know of any motels nearby? I need something not very expensive..." he said, his voice hesitant and worried.

Poor guy is probably working his way through collage, I thought, warming to his obvious nervousness.

"Have you checked out the Clarion motels? I think there is one in Marienville, but it might be too pricy for your budget."

He heaved a long sigh. "Holiday Inn, Day's Inn, they are all too expensive."

"Well, you could stay here," I said, surprised at my nerve. "My husband and I have a house in the woods and an extra bed or two."

"That would be wonderful," he said. "How do I get to your home?"

"Where are you now?" I said.

"I'm in The Paradise," he said.

My mind went blank. "The Paradise? I don't know where that is. I thought I knew all the places in the area. The Paradise?" I was stumped.

"It's on Route 66, not far from your church."

A light bulb went off in my head. I started to laugh.

"You must mean Sportsman's Paradise," I said and giggled again. "Nobody calls it The Paradise around here. It is just called *Sportsman's.*"

The more I thought about it, the more I laughed. Finally the young man laughed, too, an embarrassed laugh.

"All right," he said. I could almost see him blush.

I gave him directions to our house and he showed up later that night, after the evening's photo sessions. He and my Dave hit it off right away. They talked hunting like old pals. Best of all, he loved dogs and our great dog Sarge took to him right away. Dogs recognize good people, and Dave Peters is definitely one of the good ones.

We hosted our new friend for the several days that he spent in our area. He loved and appreciated my home cooking. We never charged him room or board. You don't ask for money from friends and Dave Peters proved to be a good friend. He visits us several times a year, always cheerful, always ready to help out any way he can.

He suffers from Muscular Dystrophy now and needs a cane to walk. His disability has not diminished his artistic talent. When my book, *Mumma's Favorite*, needed front cover art, Dave painted a beautiful picture and gave it to me. It took him months of blood, sweat and tears, but the artwork is wonderful. Funny what happens when you open your home to a stranger, right? The *Bible* urges us to be kind to strangers. Just think of all we might have missed if I had not invited Dave Peters into our home that long ago summer's day.

The first morning he sat down to homemade bread toast, my special strawberry jam, and a good strong cup of coffee he said, "So *this* is Paradise!"

Cherish Every Moment.

❦

CHAPTER 48

Maya and Sierra, Babes into Toddlers

Last Christmas season, Anna and her little family including Sierra drove up from North Carolina to Western New York to spend the holiday with Grandma Rose. Dave and I drove up on a Sunday afternoon to share an early Christmas dinner. Dave III and his children, Devin, Alex and Maya, also came over to visit. Tina, Dave's wife, had to work that day, and sadly missed all the excitement.

Maya and Sierra were born just days apart. Maya is older by six days. In fact, the previous summer, Rose and I co-hosted a family baby shower for both expectant mothers. The Moms-to-be shared the same delivery date, but Maya made her debut a week early. That snowy Sunday afternoon, the youngest of our great-granddaughters met for the first time.

The living room seemed crowded with little kids and toys. The young parents sat on the floor and watched as the girls eyeballed each other. Sierra, a sturdy toddler dressed all in pink, seemed the epitome of femininity. Maya, tall and thin, dressed in farmer's overalls over a long sleeved shirt, looked like a tough tomboy. From my perch on a recliner, I grinned as both girls went after one big blue ball.

Sierra attended daycare and had some experience with the concept of sharing. Maya had two older brothers who taught her to be tough. Both girls had two hands around the ball. Both refused to give it up, despite good-natured coaching from the sidelines.

"Come on, Sierra, share like a good girl," Adam urged.

Dave III just grinned and said nothing. The little boys watched, both were rooting for their sister Maya to come away with the ball.

After a few tense moments when tears started (Sierra), and Maya refused to give it up, the prize went to, *ta dah!* Maya.

Sierra ran to Anna and Adam for comfort, pointing toward her cousin, now holding the ball and grinning. Maya's narrow shoulders beneath the cloth suspenders were thrust back, as if to say, "*You want a piece of me? Bring it on, girly!*"

I had to laugh. When Adam scowled at me, I explained, "Maya has two older brothers. They taught her to fight for what she wants."

Sierra sat on her mother's lap and looked thoughtful. Had she learned a valuable lesson that day? Perhaps. I do know that later in the afternoon, she recaptured the blue ball and refused to let it go until all the company, including Dave III and his family, packed up and left for home.

Children, grandchildren, great-grandchildren, wonderful gifts from God. Rewards for a long life, lived with gratitude for our many blessings.

Cherish Every Moment.

CHAPTER 49

The Return of the Prodigal

Russ our second-born son was a difficult child from little up. Stubborn and more than a little lazy, he became skilled at getting his way, regardless. Slow to walk and to talk, he merely pointed and grunted when he wanted something. We had enough other children, both older and younger, to do the clean-up work, that Russ's laziness often went overlooked. Toys need picking up? *Let the other siblings do it.* No matter what punishment we doled out, no matter how often we tried to reason with him about shared responsibilities, it was always *his way or no way.*

He was a bit of a sneak, too. Often, he would arise in the middle of the night, and clean out the bread drawer, slathering homemade jam on thick slices of fresh bread, until the last of the loaf disappeared. The rest of the family would arise to find the bread drawer empty, and no bread for toast or to make sandwiches for lunch. It landed Russ in hot water more than once, believe me. But nothing we did changed his behavior.

By the time he entered his late teens, he had a big drug problem. Marijuana was his drug of choice, cheap and readily available at the local hang-outs for druggies. No matter how often we

caught him, and threatened to throw him out of the house, the
drugs continued to hold sway over his behavior. Finally when he
reached age twenty, he did something so dangerous to the safety
of his younger brother, that we were forced to make him leave.

Riding bicycles down our country road with a younger brother,
Russ waited until an approaching car came near enough, then
encouraged his brother to steer across the road into the path of
the oncoming car. The howl of brakes and a blare of car horn
alerted me. The driver stopped and came to the house. When the
driver's finger pointed at our irresponsible son, it spelled the end
of Russ's happy home. Always a survivor, Russ found another family
to take him in, drugs and all. This family had a young daughter
whom Russ loved. If we had been the parents of that young girl,
we would not have been so generous.

One day, after a year or more of silence, Russ called to tell us
he and his girl friend were now parents of a baby boy named
Tony. I congratulated him and asked, "So when is the wedding?"

Silence for a bit, then Russ said defensively, "She doesn't want
to marry me."

Gee, I wonder why? I thought, remembering his drug habits.

"Still smoking weed?" I asked dryly.

"Uh, not so much anymore. Don't have enough money to
buy it anymore."

"So, are you working? What are your plans to support your son?"

A big sigh over the phone. I wondered what else he wanted to
tell me.

"I just called to let you know I am moving to California. Already bought my bus ticket."

"Will Wendy and the baby go with you?"

Another long sigh.

"She doesn't want to leave her folks." He sighed again. "At
least it will be warm in California."

Outside the snow blew sideways across the yard. Hard hail tapped against the kitchen window.

"Well, good luck, Son. Hope you find work out there."

For all purposes, that was the last we heard from Russ for over thirty years. What went on in California remains anyone's guess. We discovered later that he lived on the streets for a time. We heard he spent some jail time for possession of drugs. At one time he tried to blow up his apartment in a vain suicide attempt. He suffered burns to the face and upper torso and spent a long time in the rehabilitation burn unit. Still, as the years went by, we knew very little of his whereabouts or how he was surviving. At different times during the thirty-year period, several of his brothers tried to track him down to no avail. It seemed he had vanished off the face of the earth. In blue moments, I pictured an unmarked grave in Mexico, product of a drug deal gone wrong.

We were living in California during part of Russ's time away from the family. My first four books were published. I had appeared on television and radio, even had publicity articles and photos in the local paper. I fantasied that he might see my name in a newspaper, or on the cover of a book, and contact us. It never happened. By the time we moved to Pennsylvania, I had given up hope of ever seeing our second son again. Sometimes Dave would mention Russ.

"I wonder just what happened to that boy."

I would shrug, helplessly. Russ was far from being an innocent boy, he would turn fifty soon. What more could we do to contact a son who obviously did not want to be found?

Then late one evening, just before Christmas, the phone rang. It was after eleven o'clock. We were already in bed. I jumped up, heart in my throat. Every parent knows the drill. *Phone call this late at night. Bad news!* But this time, the astonishing news brought warm tears of gratitude.

I did not recognize the faint voice on in my ear.

"Uh, Mom?"

"Jim?"

Our youngest son's job took him out on the road for long stretches of time. *What's wrong? Did he have an accident?*

"No, not Jim." A long sigh, a familiar sound that I should have recognized, but didn't.

"Who is it, then? Jason?"

Jason served in the Air Force in Desert Storm. Had he been called up again and deployed to Iraq?

"Are you OK? Are you hurt? Where are you?" My voice sounded shrill with worry.

"Not Jason," the voice said and finally revealed his identity. "This is Russ."

My knees buckled. "Russ?" I said, my voice squeaking. "Our *son*, Russ?"

The chuckle from our second-born son sounded as relieved as I felt.

"I was afraid you would hang up on me," he said and coughed with repressed emotion.

We were both near tears as we talked on and on. My bare toes and legs turned purple with cold as the conversation continued. Outside, the winter sky lit up with the bright Northern star.

I stared out the cold window and wept. It was two weeks before Christmas and I had just received the gift of the Magi. *Russ, our prodigal son had called. He wanted to return to the family fold.*

Cherish Every Moment.

࿎࿎࿎

CHAPTER 50

Miracle Moments to Remember

The following summer, Russ moved back East. It was not an easy adjustment for him or the rest of the family. Russ the man had not really changed that much from the self-involved boy who thought everything should be his way or no way. He managed to cajole youngest brother Jim into flying out to California to help him drive across country in his old truck.

"Russ, I'll send you a map. You don't need another driver. Jim will miss work He has a family to support, you know."

Nope. Jim had to fly out and help drive Russ home. They arrived at Jim's house in Western New York a week later. Jim went back to work and Russ moved into Jim's spare room. He did not seek employment until his small stash of money disappeared.

Jim's wife Andrea, at first willing to house and feed the Prodigal, soon became disillusioned. She complained to me over the phone.

"Mom, Russ *needs* to find a job. We can't keep supporting him forever."

"I know, Andrea." I bit my tongue before I reminded her, *I did try to warn you.*

Eventually, driven by his need to buy cigarettes, Russ did go to work, part time. He complained bitterly about never having enough money.

"You can always quit smoking, Russ."

"Yeah, right," he said sourly.

"No workee, no eatee," I reminded him. "And no smokee, either."

He wanted us to send him money. I did once, but then had to remind him of the hard reality of today's world.

"Sorry, Son," I said. "We have bills to pay, too. Welcome to the real world."

The thinking process of our difficult son has always baffled me. Why, in a family raised to be real workers, did this one son turn out to be so unmotivated? As one child seemingly lost in the hubbub of a large family, did he think that dragging his feet and refusing to work would earn him more attention? As a too-busy mother of many, Russ's thinking process always remained a mystery to me.

After Jim and Andrea tired of their boarder, Russ moved in with Mike. That didn't last long either. Eventually, he did find a place of his own and a full-time job working construction for a private contractor. Later, he branched out on his own. Now, like Adam after the fall, Russ works for his bread by the sweat of his brow. It has been a tough lesson for him. Did he think his family would take in the returned Prodigal, and, like the *Bible* story, provide him with a life of ease for the rest of his life? When the rest of the family wonders about the thought processes of their brother, I tell them, "Some people just have to learn things the hard way."

I do have hope for Russ. He is growing up, finally. Our relationship has changed from heavy-handed mother and naughty son, to two adults who can actually laugh and joke together. This is something that might never have happened if he had not moved back East. Russ the adult (finally!) is a much nicer person, than Russ the prodigal boy.

One day he called with great news.

"You'll never guess what I did today, Mom."

"Hard to tell with you, Russ," I said, teasing him a little.

He laughed. "I stopped at a church and registered as a parishioner."

I gasped. Never in a million years would I have believed this could happen!

He took my gasp as profound shock or maybe even disbelief. He hurried on to explain.

"When we all got together for that first family meal after I moved back, everybody started saying *Grace* and I stood there like a big dummy. I couldn't even remember the words!"

"But we said *Grace* the whole time you lived at home, Russ. You said that prayer before sitting down to supper, from the time you learned to talk and for the next seventeen years! How could you forget the words?"

"Must have lost some brain cells from all those drugs, ya think, Mom?"

I had to agree.

"So, what now, Russ? What did they say at that church?"

"They signed me up for a refresher course. I start next week."

I laughed, overwhelmed at this sudden gift from God. Russ, our always difficult, squirm around on the kneeler, crawl under the pews, second son, had *chosen* to go back to church!

Now I can die happy.

Cherish Every Moment.

✳ ✳ ✳

Then another miracle happened. God planned other wonders for Russ and the rest of our family. It happened over the Memorial Day weekend, 2008. Oldest son, Ravy-Davy (now a mellowed-out, mature man with grandchildren) threw his annual family reunion picnic. Everyone who attended brought a dish to pass. God blessed us with perfect weather. The sun brightened the deep green lushness of Dave's lawn and filtered through the heavy leaves of his maple trees. Groups of people sat around laughing as they talked about "the good old days" when our adult children (many are grandparents already) were young and full of spunk. Two of our old neighbors, the Schichtel brothers, were there with their wives and children. I felt showered with blessings that bright afternoon as I gazed around at our family and friends.

Thank you, God, I prayed more than once.

Then the real miracle began. Russ's son, Tony, had arrived early in the day. Although we tried to keep in touch with our grandson, Tony, from the time he was born until we moved to California, it had been several years since we last saw him. We hugged and played catch-up as we shared our picnic meal. In a strange twist of fate, Tony revealed that he works for George Schichtel, the uncle of the two brothers who were our neighbors in Eden, forty years ago.

Tony said, "Do you think Russ will come?"

I noticed that he did not call his birth father, *Dad.* Why should he? Russ had abandoned him shortly after his birth. Wendy and her parents had raised the boy as best they could, given their limited financial means. Russ never contributed child support. All his money went for drugs, apparently. We tried to help Tony by sending gifts on his birthday and Christmas. But now, here was a grown-up grandson, thirty years old, asking about his father.

I hesitated. "Russ knows about the party. He may come later. He works for an independent contractor and may be working today."

Tony ducked his head so I wouldn't see the disappointment in his Bauer-brown eyes.

Son Dave stood by the kitchen doorway, listening to our conversation. He turned quickly and went into the house. Later he told me how he phoned his brother and gave him marching orders.

"Russ, get your butt over here. Your son is here!"

No one argues with Ravy when he gets his back up!

An hour later, Russ pulled into the crowded yard and parked his truck beside our car. He climbed slowly out of the cab and stood there looking around. His face reflected uncertainty and not a little apprehension. I noticed he had showered and trimmed his usually scraggly beard.

Good! At least he is trying.

I stood beside Tony as Russ slowly approached us. Before he got within hearing distance, I said to Tony, "Your dad was just a kid when you were born. He had no sense of responsibility then. Don't judge him too harshly."

Tony, bless him, smiled and patted my arm. He, too, looked nervous. It is not every day when a man meets his birth father for the very first time.

I introduced father to son, son to father, and walked away. If they were going to yell at each other, I did *not* want to be in the middle of it. If they had fought, I would have wept.

From across the yard, sitting beside son, Mike, we watched the drama unfold. At first they scarcely glanced at each other. Both had their arms folded, protecting their hearts from further injury, maybe? I whispered to Mike, "Look at them, can you tell they are related?"

Mike chuckled and folded his arms in a mockery of the men across the yard. "Should I go over there and knock their stubborn heads together, Mom?"

When we glanced back, both Tony and Russ had unfolded their arms. They actually moved closer to each other. They began to talk, really *talk* to each other. My heart gave a great leap of gratitude.

Thank you, God!

Later, we saw the two of them go over to Russ's truck and open the hood. Turns out Tony is a good mechanic, something Russ admires, since he has no clue how to fix a vehicle.

The next day, Russ phoned to tell me about their conversation.

"I told Tony that the real reason I came back to Western New York was to meet him." His chuckle echoed over the telephone. "That snapped his head around." Russ went on and on, bragging about his son, filling my heart with renewed gratitude. "You know, Mom, that kid is smart!" Russ sounded just like a proud papa. About time!

Now we can truly die happy.

Cherish Every Moment.

Blest are We

In the cemetery of St. Mary's Church in Crown, Pennsylvania, our double-heart headstone awaits us. I feel it is fitting, somehow, that our final resting place is only a few hundred yards from the place where we began our lifetime journey together, at the Crown dance. When we decided to move from California in 1995, we picked Pennsylvania instead of Western New York (where we raised our family), for our last retirement home. We both felt our rural roots calling us. Dave's people help settle this region and so did my ancestors. In the cemetery at Crown, our plot is not far from Dave's parents' graves. My grandparents' and many great-grandparents' remains rest peacefully nearby. We came home to be with our kin.

When we made our pre-funeral arrangements last summer, we ordered a double-heart pink granite marker engraved with our names, birth dates, and date of our wedding. In a smaller heart, we chose the words, *Blest Are We,* to remind our family just how blessed we have always been. Blessed with a house full of children, blessed with a long-lived love, blessed to live long enough to see our grandchildren and great-grandchildren. Through bad times and great times, poor times and times of abundance, sickness and health, times of loss and times of rebirth, one thing has remained a constant: God's never failing love and care for all our needs.

Blest Are We!
Trust God and laugh every day!
Most of all: *Cherish Every Moment!*

Printed in the United States
220853BV00001B/15/P